design ideas for
Bathrooms

CREATIVE HOMEOWNER®, Upper Saddle River, New Jersey

VP, Editorial Director: Timothy O. Bakke
Production Manager: Kimberly H. Vivas
Managing Editor: Fran Donegan
Senior Editor: Kathie Robitz
Editorial Assistants: Evan Lambert (Proofreading);
    Lauren Manoy (Photo Research)
Senior Designer: Glee Barre
Author: Susan Boyle Hillstrom
Photography (unless otherwise noted): Mark Samu
Cover Photographs: *(top)* courtesy of Toto; *(bottom left)*
    courtesy of Corian; *(bottom center)* courtesy of
    DEX Studios
Inside Front Cover Photographs: *(top)* Design: Correia
    Designs, Ltd.
Back Cover Photography: *(top)* courtesy of Merillat;
    (bottom left) Tony Giammarino; *(bottom center)*
    courtesy of Ceramic Tile of Italy; *(bottom right)* courtesy
    of Sonoma Cast Stone
Inside Back Cover Photography: Design: Lee Najman
Cover Design: Glee Barre

Current Printing (last digit)
10 9 8 7 6 5 4 3 2

Printed in China

Design Ideas for Bathrooms
Library of Congress Control Number: 2004114553
ISBN: 1-58011-234-X

CREATIVE HOMEOWNER®
A Division of Federal Marketing Corp.
24 Park Way
Upper Saddle River, NJ 07458
www.creativehomeowner.com

Dedication

To my father, Vilas J. Boyle, who got me started.

Acknowledgments

Many thanks to Kathie Robitz, the perfect editor, for being helpful, encouraging, smart, and funny. And to the art staff, senior designer, Glee Barre, and photo researcher, Lauren Manoy, who made a beautiful book. Thanks also to my husband, Roger Hillstrom, for providing encouragement, support—and dinner.

Contents

ABOVE Tempered-glass shower doors keep handsome stone tilework on view.

RIGHT A custom vanity is part of a suite of cabinetry designed for this room.

BELOW In the same bathroom, the tilework is carried over to the backsplash and tub surround.

Bathrooms are complex spaces, made up of many elements that must work together smoothly to ensure comfort, convenience, and safety. And now this once strictly utilitarian space has become a "designer" room. You'll want every bath in your house to be beautiful, especially the master bathroom. This will be your serene retreat from daily life, filled with as many amenities as your budget allows.

If you have bought *Design Ideas for Bathrooms*, you are embarking on some kind of bathroom project—or at least thinking about it. It may be a simple facelift, a major remodeling, or the construction of an

Introduction

entirely new space. Whatever your goal, you'll be grateful that you have found this guide through the dizzying world of trends and the staggering number of available products. The pages that follow will introduce you to all of the elements you must consider—fixtures, fittings, surface materials, cabinets, lighting, and ventilation systems. The information, tips, and bright ideas supplied will help you plan your project and decide which products best meet your needs, taste, and budget. As you study the collection of photographs, you'll find the inspiration you need to make your design dreams become reality.

Unless you are older than 30—or live in a house that is older than 40—you may not remember how boring and dysfunctional bathrooms used to be. Once cramped and inefficient, older baths generally contained an unimaginative arrangement of toilet, sink, tub, and maybe a shower; yet in the typical one-bath house of the time, they had to serve the whole family. Happily, the boring bath is a thing of the past. Today's baths are functional and good-looking, and often equipped with luxurious health-club amenities. Here are a few ideas for a new or revitalized bath of your own.

Begin with the Basics

I planned to be personal I formulate ideas
I work with space I master baths I
I family baths I half-baths I
I universal design I

Today's oasis-like bathrooms often center on a large tub for sybaritic soaking. This one, in a prime position to capture treetop views, adjoins a capacious shower.

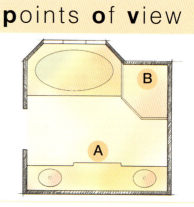

LEFT AND ABOVE One-of-a kind touches in this bath include an elaborate vanity with fine-furniture details, and a mosaic-tile mural in the shower.

planned

points **o**f **v**iew

RIGHT AND MIDDLE In another bath, French-style fittings look glamorous with a satisfyingly spacious tub.

OPPOSITE TOP The sealed-wood deck holds soaps and towels.

OPPOSITE BOTTOM A separate grooming area adjoins the main bath.

points **o**f **v**iew

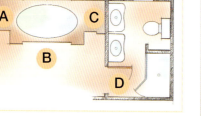

Today's home probably contains a couple of bathrooms, maybe more—a powder room conveniently near activity areas, a bath just for kids or especially for guests, and of course, the queen of them all, the master bath. In many cases, it is also a designer room, with decorating schemes that reflect personal tastes and with equipment that suits individual needs and the desire for pampering. Do you dream of a luxurious soak at the end of the day? Whatever your budget or space situation, there is a tub to make that fantasy come true. If you prefer showering, your choices are also varied, from a compact corner unit to a spacious spa-like stall with steam capability. It's the same story with sinks, toilets, and faucets—they all range

to be **personal**

from serviceable to sybaritic, and from cost-conscious to pricey.

When it comes to the look of the bath, you can get really personal. Fixtures, fittings, surfacing materials, and accessories, available in many sizes, shapes, colors, and styles, let you easily create whatever look you like. Go sleek and contemporary, or cozy and traditional, in the master bath; or create a Victorian look with vintage-style fixtures. You can let yourself go in a kids' bath with whimsical faucets, colorful tiles, and playful accessories that make the room cheerful and appealing. And a powder room is the perfect place for drama and glamour. Skylights over the tub, a window in the shower, and access to a private garden or patio are other ways to personalize.

whatever your style—comfort is the key

ABOVE LEFT A variation on the Victorian footed tub and an antiqued towel rack add period flavor.

ABOVE In the same bath, rich dark-stained cabinets also recall nineteenth-century splendor.

LEFT Up-to-date amenities—a huge mirror and a two-sink vanity—coexist with traditional-style elements.

points of view

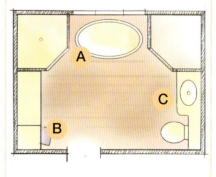

points of view

design pros

what each pro knows

- **Architects** plan, design, and oversee new construction and major remodels. You will need one if your project involves an addition or an extensive makeover of existing space.
- **Certified Bath Designers (CBD)** are schooled in all aspects of bathroom design, from layouts to equipment and materials to wiring and plumbing. Before choosing one, make sure your design sensibilities mesh.
- **Interior designers** work to create a functional and aesthetically pleasing interior. They may provide floor plans and renderings; plan lighting; advise about color; assist in the selection and purchase of materials, products, and fixtures; and monitor installation.
- **General contractors** usually work from plans drawn up by other professionals. They will get permits, install cabinets, and oversee the work of the electrician and other trades. Some specialize in bathrooms, and some work in partnership with designers.

ABOVE Sleek cabinets, a streamlined window treatment, and general restraint of embellishment visually expand space in this modest-sized bath.

BELOW With doors open, this enclosure acts as a pass-through from one part of the master suite to the other. With doors closed, it becomes a shower with a built-in bench, an adjustable showerhead, and a handheld sprayer.

RIGHT In an opulent master bath, the whirlpool tub, set on a platform in a niche of its own, reigns supreme.

RIGHT BOTTOM A large Palladian-style window ushers sunlight into the makeup area. In this elegantly appointed room, floors are tumbled marble, counters are granite.

pampered

Consider a custom steam shower or a freestanding unit with all of the trimmings. If adding such luxury will put you over budget, consider a steam unit for a tub-and-shower combination or an economical steam generator for your existing shower stall.

ABOVE The height of luxury—a frameless, clear-glass shower enclosure doubles as a steam room.

ABOVE RIGHT A gas fireplace is the owners' favorite luxury—it fires up quickly to keep the space toasty year-round.

BELOW An interior transom window brightens the tub alcove; the quilt-like mural is crafted from pieces of tumbled marble.

bright idea

saving grace

A soaking tub, in which you luxuriate in chin-deep water, is a money-saving alternative to a whirlpool.

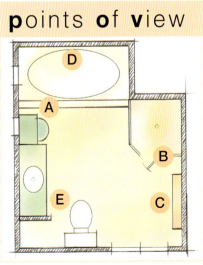

points **o**f **v**iew

oday's bathrooms are variously described as beautiful, luxurious, relaxing, even romantic. But let's not forget functional. The bath is a hard-working and complex room, and must be planned with careful attention to such practical matters as layout, safety, storage, durability, and maintenance. Sure, picking out fixtures, finishes, and colors is fun. But before you start shopping, think about some basics—what kind of bath are you planning? Who will use it? What features will it include? How much space is available? How much can you spend? To keep costs manageable, make use of existing space somewhere in your house if you can. Adding on could put you over budget.

formulate ideas

Once you have established the basics, draw up a wish list, then pare it down as space and budget dictate. Paging through design books, home-improvement magazines, and catalogs, and visiting home centers and showrooms will give you an idea of the fixtures and fittings available in your price range. Think about storage, too. If possible, aim for a variety of storage units—base cabinets with several drawer sizes, open shelves, tall cupboards for linens. Finishing materials are also important. Choose durable, moisture-resistant, and easy-to-clean surfaces. Last but not least, assure safety with good lighting and adequate ventilation to prevent the buildup of mold or mildew.

LEFT AND CENTER LEFT In a renovated bath, existing nooks and crannies separate function. One alcove becomes a water closet; another holds the tub. OPPOSITE FAR LEFT Period-style fixtures add vintage charm.

and work out details

LEFT The fundamental simplicity of this design is enlivened by nostalgic additions, most notably the reproduction console-style sink with a marble top and built-in glass towel bars.

RIGHT Nickel-plated faucets with porcelain inserts were fashionable in turn-of-the-last-century bathrooms. These reproductions blend beautifully with the style of the sink.

RIGHT BELOW A marble shelf with a gracefully beveled edge matches the sink deck and holds sundries elegantly.

OPPOSITE BOTTOM Reflected in the large, space-expanding mirror—a shelf for towels and hooks for robes and other essentials, all placed within easy reach of the shower.

LEFT TOP Lots of glass and a pale color scheme expand visual space in this bath.

LEFT CENTER This space-savvy design tucks the toilet under a slanted roofline.

LEFT In a long, narrow bath, a shower is recessed into the wall opposite the vanity.

work with space

Is space tight in your new or remodeled bath? Try some simple, space-stretching strategies to make it look and feel larger. Small-scale fixtures, for example, are as functional as their full-size cousins but save significant amounts of space. Excellent examples are sinks and toilets that are designed to fit into a small corner. Natural light is a great space-expander, too—if possible add a skylight or enlarge existing windows. Then resist the impulse to hang fussy curtains. Leave the windows unadorned or put up simple blinds if privacy is an issue. A white or pale color scheme, even on the floor, will also make the room look bigger, as will large expanses of mirror. Finally, create the illusion of greater floor space by ditching the vanity in favor of a pedestal or console-style sink. On the other hand, if the space is awkward or oddly shaped, look for ways to work with it. Make use of knee walls by building storage into them, or tuck the toilet or tub under an eave.

LEFT This stunning and ingenious arrangement of windows and skylights dramatizes a bathing corner. The natural light that pours in makes the room appear much larger than it actually is.

RIGHT A tub that has been fitted under the eaves in a remodeled attic becomes a serene sanctuary in white. Windows in the low wall are set at eye level and left unadorned for the bather, permitting views of a private woodsy setting behind the house.

bright idea

cornered

Placing this vanity in the corner allowed space for amenities—an extra counter and a window seat— on either side of it.

ABOVE In a compartmentalized bath, the toilet occupies a far corner and sinks are set on opposite walls, an ideal arrangement for two.

LEFT "Her" grooming corner boasts a makeup table with an upholstered bench and plentiful storage.

OPPOSITE BOTTOM In this room, an entire corner is devoted to a super-sized shower. Small drawers in the storage cabinet to the left are perfect for sundries or lingerie.

divide and conquer

A shared bath works best as a series of separate compartments—a water closet for the toilet, a freestanding shower, a tub alcove, and self-contained sinks. Providing these islands of privacy and preventing traffic jams is easier in a large room, but clever placement of fixtures or the addition of short walls or partitions can divide and conquer modest dimensions, too.

RIGHT A half wall of tile between the tub and makeup table separates one function from another and provides a bit of privacy.

FAR RIGHT A separate shower, once a luxury, is now standard equipment in many baths, and a necessity for a space that two people regularly use at the same time. This large version can also be equipped with steam or jets.

ABOVE In this small bath, a wall behind the tub creates a private nook for the toilet.

RIGHT Opposite the tub in the same bath—two space-saving pedestal sinks and a built-in shower.

points of view

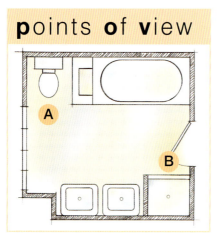

points of view

compartments increase functionality ▌

ABOVE RIGHT In a narrow space, the water closet, or "toileting room," is at one end behind a frosted-glass door.

BELOW Mirrors around the tub visually widen the long stretch of space. A shower is tucked into the corner at the other end.

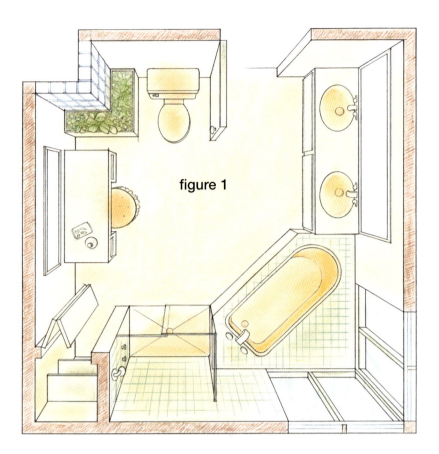

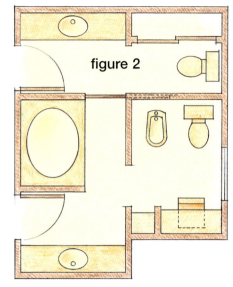

FIGURE ONE An angled bathtub conserves floor space and allows for a double vanity.

FIGURE TWO An adjacent half bath boosts a master bath's use.

finding a place for an at-home oasis

FIGURE THREE
A grand layout provides two separate but connected bathrooms within a large master suite.

FIGURE FOUR His and her zones open via pocket doors to a shared tub.

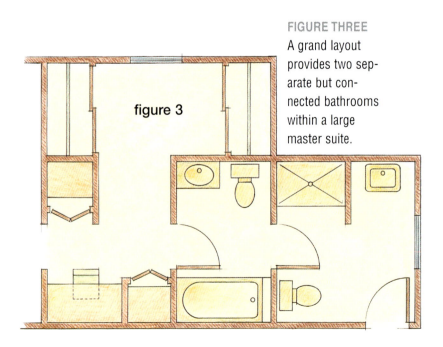

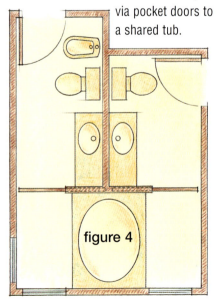

master baths

Often sequestered in a corner or wing of the house, today's master bath is part of an entire suite, an ensemble of rooms that includes a bedroom, dressing area, perhaps a sitting area, and sometimes even a deck, balcony, or private garden. But what if you don't happen to have a wing to spare? Must you give up the dream of an at-home sanctuary where you can escape the hubbub of the household and unwind from the tensions of the workday? You can build an addition to your house, of course, but this is the most expensive way to go and may put you over budget. Before you commit to that course, look around for existing usable space that can be converted into a bigger and better bath, keeping in mind that even a few square feet can make an important difference. For example, you may be able to expand a bath that adjoins your current bedroom by borrowing space from a bedroom or nearby hall closet, or the hall itself. If you have a big bedroom, you might consider sacrificing some of its square footage to enlarge the bath. Another idea—transform part, or all, of an adjacent and seldom-used bed into a master bath. This approach would work especially well for empty-nesters with room to spare. And don't overlook the possibility of annexing the attic—with a little imaginative remodeling, it could become the new and luxuriously private master suite you have always wanted.

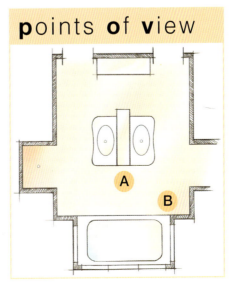

points of view

TOP The highlight of this master bath is a roomy whirlpool tub surrounded by windows.

LEFT A nifty idea for a two-person bathroom —his and her console-style sinks located on opposite sides of a partial wall.

RIGHT A well-lit corner is a perfect spot for a makeup center.

BELOW AND OPPOSITE Planned for privacy, the layout places the shower and water closet on either side of the tub, with two sinks in a separate zone.

points **o**f **v**iew

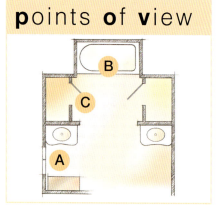

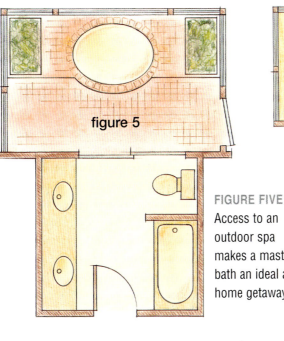

figure 5

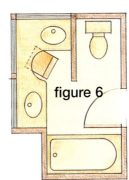

figure 6

FIGURE SIX An L-shaped countertop can make way for a pair of sinks as well as a dressing table.

FIGURE SEVEN A separate grooming area is more efficient shared space.

FIGURE FIVE Access to an outdoor spa makes a master bath an ideal at-home getaway.

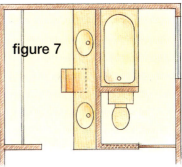

figure 7

careful planning creates islands of privacy

C

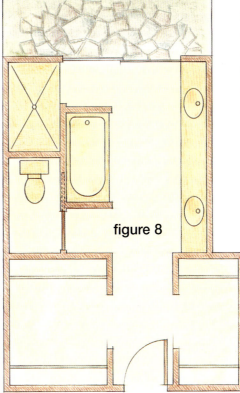

FIGURE EIGHT A pocket door conceals a water closet in this floor plan of compartmentalized zones.

figure 8

family baths

Unlike master suites, which are used by only one or two people, family baths may have to service adults, children, and senior citizens; and they require a plan that is flexible and convenient for everyone. To prevent long lines from forming outside the bathroom door on busy mornings, arrange the room for simultaneous use by more than one person with at least a modicum of privacy. For example, use some of the space to create a private toilet compartment; then place the tub and shower in one part of the room and vanity in another, allowing one person to brush her teeth while another is showering. Circumvent clutter by building in plenty of storage—cabinets, open shelves, and robe and towel hooks will help stow everybody's stuff.

beat bathroom gridlock with a multitask layout

ABOVE Used mostly by kids, this bath boasts bright primary colors and a playful tile mosaic. Ceramic-tile walls and floors wipe clean easily.

ABOVE LEFT A checkerboard-tile pattern enlivens this shower stall custom-designed for grooming the family dog, and the controls are just the right height.

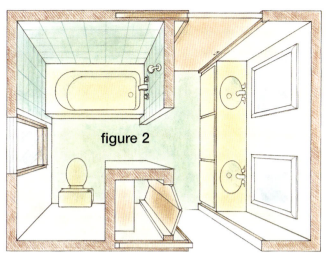

FIGURE TWO Pocket doors, installed around this room, do not use up floor space, allowing an improved floor plan.

LEFT This family-friendly layout includes a long vanity with separate sinks and mirrors for busy mornings.

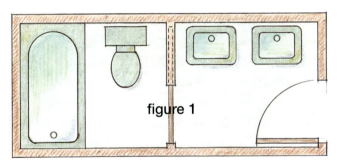

FIGURE ONE Locating the sinks, which are the most-used fixtures, nearest the door is logical.

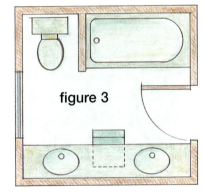

FIGURE THREE A partition next to the toilet expands the use of a bathroom without a costly addition.

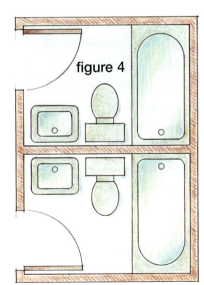

FIGURE FOUR Back-to-back plumbing creates two smaller bathrooms from one formerly large space.

LEFT In the same bath, the tub is sequestered in a far corner, overlooking a soothing view of fields and treetops.

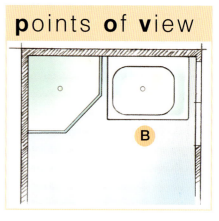

points of view

A

points of view

B

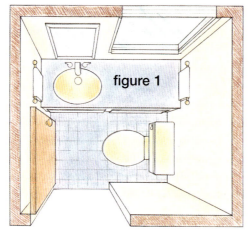

FIGURE ONE A large vanity is helpful if a half bath doubles as an extra grooming area on busy mornings.

ABOVE Regularly used by guests, powder rooms should be pretty. In this one, a handsome mirror sits above a distressed wood table that serves as the vanity.

RIGHT A shower turns a half bath into a three-quarter bath. A deep utility sink and arched faucet is convenient for rinsing hand-washable items.

B

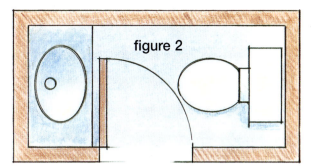

Furnished with only a sink and toilet, half-baths are handy little spaces. Used as powder rooms for the convenience of guests, they are typically placed on the first floor near public areas. If possible, create a sense of privacy for your guests by positioning a powder room so that it does not open immediately onto a living room, dining room, family room, or wherever people will congregate in your household. Find a spot in the front hall or around the corner from activity areas.

Although guests generally don't linger in powder rooms, these diminutive spaces do get a lot of use, especially if you entertain often. Don't skimp on quality; instead, invest in fixtures that can be counted on to work efficiently over time. If space is especially tight, investigate small-scale fixtures. A pedestal sink consumes less floor area than a sink-vanity combination; but to compensate for the loss of a vanity counter, install a shelf to hold soaps and guests' makeup paraphernalia. Be sure to include a mirror with lighting.

Other likely places for a half-bath are near a guest bedroom, in a finished basement, off the kitchen, or in the bedroom wing to supplement a family bath.

half-baths

FIGURE TWO In a long narrow room, place the toilet and the sink on opposite walls.

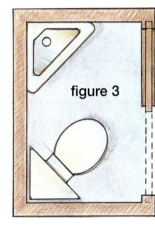

FIGURE THREE Corner fixtures and a pocket door are small-space solutions.

pint-sized rooms with big-time impact

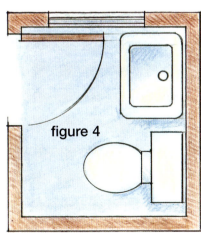

FIGURE FOUR Locate the sink and the toilet on the same wall to conserve floor space.

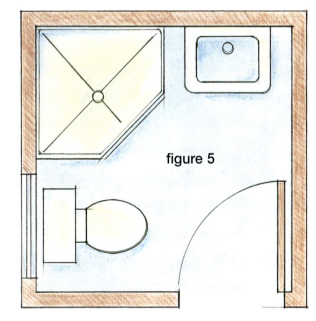

FIGURE FIVE A corner shower unit can convert a half-bath into a three-quarter bath.

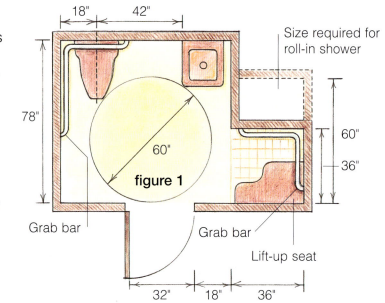

FIGURE ONE Two types of showers are geared for wheelchair use. People who can leave the wheelchair can move onto the seat of a small shower. If the person must remain in the wheelchair while bathing, a roll-in shower must be installed (indicated by dashed lines).

make the room accessible for all

A few decades ago, bathroom designers and product manufacturers awoke to the fact that bathrooms need to be not only safe for all members of the family but also accessible for all people, of all levels of physical abilities. The result was Universal Design, which assures safety, convenience, and maneuverability for anyone who uses the bath.

universal design

To accommodate people with limited mobility or poor eyesight, designers suggest placing grab bars in strategic places—around the tub, toilet, and shower—installing lever-style faucets, and making sure lights are bright in every corner of the room, particularly the shower. Swing-open doors present problems for wheelchair users. Make access easier by replacing a conventional door with a pocket door; if space permits, allow enough of an area in the center of the room for a wheelchair to turn around. Some manufacturers produce bathtubs and sinks that cater to wheelchair users, and showers with built-in seats are also available. Install a flat-threshold shower compartment that won't obstruct entry by a wheelchair.

While you're planning your new bath, why not incorporate some ease-of-use features that you might appreciate in the future if not now? Consider easy-grip C-shaped cabinet hardware, nonslip floors or mats in tub and shower, and scald-protection faucets. A light switch outside the bathroom door might also be helpful.

bright idea

safety first

Grab bars in bathtubs and showers are helpful for people of any age or physical ability.

OPPOSITE TOP There is knee room under this accessible sink. Lever-handle faucets are easiest to use.

OPPOSITE BOTTOM Grab bars reduce the risk of slipping and injuring yourself when standing up in the tub.

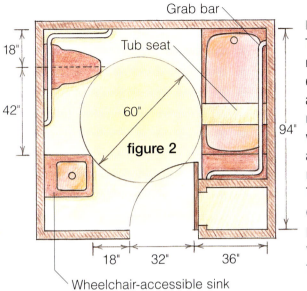

Grab bar

Tub seat

60"

figure 2

18"
42"
94"

18"   32"   36"

Wheelchair-accessible sink

FIGURE TWO
These are the minimum clearances and accessories required for wheelchair access in a bathroom with a tub. The 60-in. clear circle allows a person in a wheelchair to turn around.

The refreshing and restorative qualities of water are powerful, whether we soak in it or stand under streams of it. And when it's time to equip your bathroom, you'll find that many types of "water experiences" are available. Are you typically in a hurry to get on with your day? Then you may be happy with a no-frills tub or shower. But if you've got the time or the desire for some relaxation, you'll be interested in today's pampering soaking tubs, spa-like whirlpools, and fully loaded showers. Here, we have gathered all types of bathing options, from simple to sumptuous, for your consideration.

Bath and Shower

❙ bathtubs ❙ showers ❙
❙ fittings ❙

Treat yourself to pampering amenities that can enhance your enjoyment of a new bathtub or shower.

bath

OPPOSITE This tub's stone platform is large enough to accommodate soaps, towels, and reading material.

OPPOSITE BOTTOM LEFT AND RIGHT These drop-in tubs, both set in marble-tiled surrounds, are positioned to over-look peaceful views.

RIGHT Decorative tile insets give this alcove tub extra personality.

BELOW RIGHT A claw-foot tub sets the stage for a Victorian-style room.

S izes, shapes, and features vary, but there are only a few basic types of bathtubs in terms of installation. Placed against walls on three sides, *alcove,* or *recessed,* tubs are the most common. *Free-standing* tubs may have feet, legs, or a pedestal. *Drop-in* tubs are installed inside a platform or a fin-ished surround.

tubs

The most common tub materi-als include fiberglass, which is lightweight and inexpen-sive but shows scratches and other types of wear. High-quality acrylic is lightweight, too—essential if you're selecting an extra-large tub—but more durable. Fiberglass and acrylic can be molded into dif-ferent shapes. Porcelain or enamel over cast iron is almost in-destructible, but it's heavy. Porce-lain or enamel over steel is fairly lightweight, but it can chip and rust. Less common examples in–clude sophisticated—and de-manding—copper, stainless steel, teak, concrete, and stone.

shopping for a tub

How much can you spend? How much space do you have? A one-piece tub and shower unit can cost as little as $300; a tub with fancy spa features can set you back several thousand dollars or more. You can save a bundle by selecting only those features you really want—and will use.

Five-foot-long alcove tubs or corner models work well in small spaces; freestanding tubs and large whirlpools may be as much as 7 ft. long and 5 ft. wide. If you're remodeling, size matters: some models may not fit through existing doors and hallways. Weight is important, too. Large tubs filled with lots of water may need additional floor support.

The bottom line is buy the best tub you can afford. Test it in the showroom. Make sure that it's comfortable and that you can get in and out of it easily.

LEFT Located in a sunny bay, this drop-in tub takes on an air of luxury.

BELOW A tub and shower combination can look glamorous in a tiled alcove.

cozy alcove tubs are ideal for small spaces

OPPOSITE TOP
A standard-size tub conserves floor space in a modest-size room.

OPPOSITE RIGHT
A beadboard backsplash adds character and complements the wood-panel tub surround.

OPPOSITE FAR RIGHT A glass door permits a view of the handsomely tiled wall inside the bath alcove.

bright idea

true grit

For a safer, less-slippery surface, use small tiles with plenty of grout lines for gritty traction.

bathtub **s**afety

With its potentially slippery surfaces and unforgiving materials, your beautiful new bathroom can be a hazardous place. However, you can prevent mishaps.

❚ Buy a tub with a nonslip, textured bottom.

❚ Select a tub that you can get into and out of easily and that has controls or fixtures in an accessible location.

❚ Be aware that step-up platforms may be risky. Experts recommend no more than one step, which should be less than 7 in. high and at least 10 in. deep.

❚ Place solidly anchored grab bars with textured, easy-grip surfaces in a couple of strategic places on the tub wall or deck.

❚ Choose antiscald faucets with easy-turn lever-style handles.

❚ Use ground-fault circuit interrupters (GFCI) on outlets and moisture-proof fixtures near the tub.

ABOVE RIGHT An extra-deep Japanese-inspired soaking tub, with jets, is enclosed in a stone surround. Its placement in a windowed corner with views of nearby woods promises a serene bathing experience.

OPPOSITE TOP LEFT Mirrors and an expanse of glass block magnify the feeling of space around this recessed drop-in tub.

OPPOSITE TOP RIGHT Columns and a marble-tile surround heighten the drama of a large whirlpool in this master bathroom.

OPPOSITE BOTTOM LEFT A semicircular bay of windows is devoted to bathing and features an oval tub that has been set into a mosaic-tile step-up platform.

OPPOSITE BOTTOM RIGHT A molded acrylic whirlpool tub sits serenely in a corner.

BELOW Based on vintage designs, today's updated pedestal tubs are elegant and deep enough to guarantee a relaxing soak.

ABOVE RIGHT Beautifully painted and reglazed, this vintage claw-foot tub is ready for another century of use.

ABOVE LEFT A brand-new pedestal tub with a hand-painted base looks refined with brass fittings and matching brass-trimmed towel rails.

LEFT AND OPPOSITE BOTTOM These two designs, created by French modernist designer Philippe Starck, offer a minimalist take on Victorian tubs. The tub on the left rests on the floor, while the one on the opposite page stands on wooden feet.

refinish or **r**eplace?

Old bathtubs may show signs of wear and tear eventually, or the color fades or becomes outdated. Then comes the decision—refinish or replace?

▌ **Replacing.** A new tub is not necessarily expensive, but factor in the cost of installing it (after removing the old one) and the cost goes up. After you have shut off the water supply to the tub and fished out the drain and overflow assembly, you've got to separate the tub from the wall and the floor, which may require some demolition. If you're removing a standard 30- x 60-in. tub, you may be able to carry it out sideways through doors and hallways, or even through a window. Another solution may be to break up the tub with a saw or sledgehammer, a messy, time-consuming task.

▌ **Refinishing.** Some of the hassle involved in replacing a tub can make refinishing a better idea if your old one is in fairly good condition. Professionals can repair minor chips and cracks in enameled or porcelainized tubs and reglaze the surface. The refurbishing will last about 5 years. Another somewhat longer-lasting solution is a tub liner. This involves applying a form-fitting acrylic sheet, or liner, over the old tub. The liner is fabricated from one of literally hundreds of molds made of standard old tubs. The installer takes detailed measurements of your tub to make a seamless match. Upon installation, a special adhesive binds the liner to the tub without disturbing the adjacent walls and existing plumbing.

spa-style bathtubs take pampering to dazzling heights

LEFT This 5-ft.-long "spa/massage" tub lets you choose the kind of bath that suits your mood—from gentle bubbles to a vigorous massage. A chromotherapy option lights up the water in a variety of soothing colors.

OPPOSITE BOTTOM You can immerse yourself in this 25-in.-deep "overflowing" tub. You'll feel like you're floating in a mineral stream as water seems to cascade over the sides. (Actually, the water is recirculated.)

RIGHT Set in a gleaming granite platform and facing distant views, this tub offers the ultimate in relaxation.

BELOW In a sleek contemporary setting, a soaking tub with overflow and chromotherapy features sits next to a walk-in shower.

showers

Some people prefer the efficient, invigorating experience of a shower to a slow soak in a tub. And there are plenty of features to make showering just as special and luxurious. In fact, the feature-filled shower is so popular that in some households it has replaced the tub altogether.

The most common, most economical—and least convenient—shower is the one that's combined with the

bathtub. If you've stepped in and out of the tub, done battle with the shower curtain, or tried to keep a shower door clean, you'll be aware that a separate shower enclosure is a luxury in itself, filled with extra features or not.

You'll need space—and a hefty budget—for a large luxury shower, but some compact models are quite reasonable. Fiberglass or acrylic prefabricated units are generally 73 inches high and 36 inches deep; typical widths are 32, 36, or 48 inches. Don't let the word "prefabricated" fool you. True, some of these units are very basic, equipped with no more than a standard showerhead and a little soap dish. But other prefabricated models offer luxury features such as multiple showerheads, body sprays, jets, steam capabilities, chromotherapy options, TVs, and DVD and CD players.

Custom-designed showers often boast similar luxury features, but their enclosures are usually more luxurious, with walls covered in stone, ceramic tiles, or, in some contemporary bathrooms, even glass, metal, or concrete.

ABOVE LEFT Part of an attic that was converted into a master suite, this custom-built shower is tucked under the eaves and tiled in soft-blue ceramic squares.

OPPOSITE BOTTOM This sleek shower enclosure is lined with mosaic tiles in a blue shade that is reminiscent of the ocean. A fringe benefit of using mosaics on the shower floor—the many grout lines enhance traction.

ABOVE This bathroom offers the best of both bathing worlds—just steps away from the luxurious tub is a glamorous shower. The glass enclosure keeps the handsome granite tiles on display.

RIGHT Even a bathroom of modest dimensions can accommodate a deluxe walk-in shower. This space-saving corner design is filled with such amenities as a built-in bench, handheld sprayers, and adjustable showerheads. The glass enclosure keeps the shower from overpowering the room.

glamorous spa showers

more water?

Today's shower amenities are very appealing, but to function properly, spa features such as body sprays and jets require an adequate water supply, without which your luxurious "water experience" might be abruptly curtailed. Talk to your plumber about a larger or additional water heater or a booster pump, or check out low-flow body sprays that use less water to pamper you.

OPPOSITE TOP LEFT A curved, extra-large shower enclosure offers separate controls for body sprays and temperature. There's no need for a towel—warm-air jets dry you off in a jiffy.

OPPOSITE TOP RIGHT A compact steam shower with a molded-in bench, body sprays, and hydrotherapy jets offers big luxury for small spaces.

LEFT Custom made and luxurious in marble, this glass-enclosed shower is equipped with steam.

RIGHT This simple but spacious prefabricated angled module is made of a molded high-gloss acrylic. It comes in several pieces that easily fit through standard-size doorways, alleviating delivery concerns.

ABOVE Cross-handle-style controls have a simple utilitarian look to them that goes well with this spare, contemporary setting.

LEFT The oil-rubbed brushed bronze finish on this tub set blends well with the colors in this traditional bathroom, especially the honey tone wood cabinetry.

BELOW Lever handles are an especially good choice for children or seniors.

LEFT Copper accents make these polished-chrome fittings both sophisticated and elegant.

BELOW Often called "French telephone" style because of its shape, this polished-chrome vintage-style tub set boasts cross handles and a body sprayer, all trimmed with white enamel.

fittings

The beautification of the bathroom extends to every element, right down to the fittings. As a result, today's faucets are good-looking, durable, and hassle free. New washerless models won't drip, and brass valves won't wear out. But beware of lightweight faucets with plastic parts. They do wear out—quickly. For the tub, you'll need to choose between wall-mount or deck-mount fittings. Choices abound for finishes and styles, too. Chrome is the most familiar, but brass, nickel, bronze, pewter, and enamels are also popular. Brushed or satin matte finishes are easier to maintain because, unlike glossy polished finishes, they don't show scratches and water spots as easily. Styles range from Victorian to traditional to sleek and modern. For design continuity, make sure all fittings harmonize with one another and with the overall design of the room.

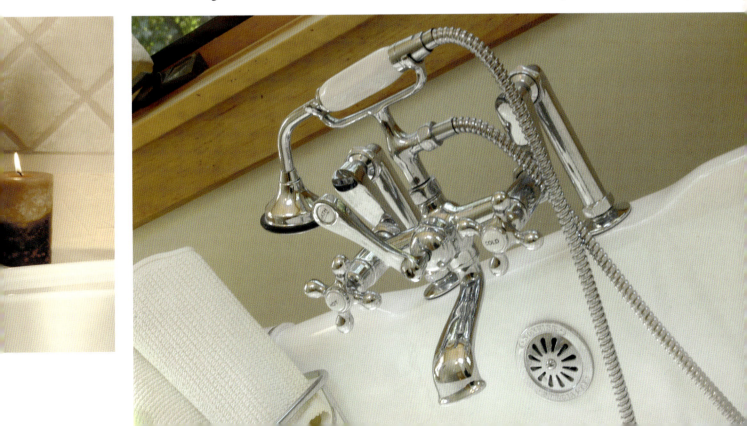

LEFT Geared to the needs of its owners, this custom shower includes a hand-held sprayer and hydro-massage jets.

RIGHT This large showerhead delivers a gentle, rain-like spray of water.

BELOW LEFT Turn the controls and water cascades from this brushed-copper shower bar.

RIGHT The brushed-bronze finish on this showerhead, diverter, and spout is both elegant and low-maintenance.

OPPOSITE A hydro-massage system features five adjustable body-spray jets and a showerhead with multiple settings.

showerhead settings

There's no such thing as a boring shower these days—at least there doesn't need to be. Even reasonably priced single shower-heads come with two or more special features—massaging, pulsating sprays that pound muscles to relieve soreness, refreshing cascades of water, or gentle flows that feel like a summer rain. Hand-held sprays, also reasonably priced, direct a stream of water exactly where you want it to go and usually offer a choice of spray settings. Sophisticated style comes at all price levels, too.

Multiple showerheads kick things up several notches. Positioned at different heights on the shower wall, they direct the water at the shoulders, lower-back, and thigh area, providing a stand-up whirlpool massage. In some showers, jets can be placed on more than one wall to create a whole "body spa." If you can't afford in-the-wall jets, check out the retrofitted unit, below.

bright idea
frugal fix

Want to bring your bathroom up to date without breaking the budget? Retrofit that boring old tub with a compact jetted bar that provides a spa-like water massage.

heat your spa's floor

Treat yourself to even more pampering—underfoot. Traditional radiant-heating systems consist of hot-water-carrying pipes embedded in a concrete slab. The water warms the concrete, which radiates heat into the room. It is expensive, but efficient. A new version of radiant heating, electric systems do away with the piping and slab, allowing you to bring radiant heat to a smaller area, such as your bathroom. Available from a number of manufacturers, the systems consist of a mesh that contains a heating element, pictured below. All you have to do is staple the mesh to the subfloor, and then apply ceramic tile in thinset. Most systems are used as auxiliary heating.

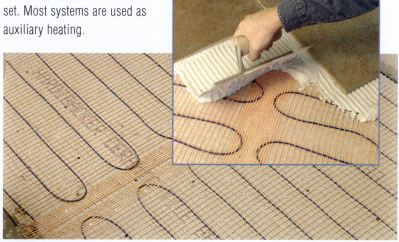

BELOW Geared for one-person soaking, this drop-in hot tub is 25 in. deep and includes eight water-massage jets.

RIGHT Installed in a walk-in shower, a 10-jet body spa aims streams of water at the entire length of your body for an invigorating hydro-massage. A chromotherapy option creates the illusion of color in the water.

OPPOSITE BOTTOM LEFT A bright idea borrowed from European hotels, heated racks have warm towels ready for you when you step out of the bath or shower. This one plugs into a wall receptacle, but some are hard-wired into the wall.

OPPOSITE BOTTOM RIGHT A metal bracket swivels so that you can enjoy this 13-in. TV even while soaking in the tub.

spa **a**menities

There are many ways to make your bathroom truly luxurious. You might break the budget if you choose every one of them. Otherwise, aim for affordable luxury by splurging on one or two favorite features, such as

▮ A TV that's visible from the tub—relax and watch a movie while you soak.

▮ A CD player in the shower—pick the tunes that rev your spirits in the morning or relax you at night.

▮ Shower jets that target specific muscles—get a massage whenever you ache.

▮ A built-in tanning feature—keep skin moist by tanning while you shower.

▮ Access to the outdoors. Equip an adjacent deck or patio with a hot tub you can use year-round.

Ideally, the floors, walls, and countertops in your bathroom perform two important services at the same time—they establish the stylish look of your choice, and they provide easy-clean surfaces that stand up to wear and tear and resist moisture and humidity. There are many materials from which to chose—stone, ceramic tile, glass, concrete, solid-surfacing, plastic laminate, wood, and metal—and most of them come in a mind-boggling choice of sizes, shapes, and colors. The following information and portfolio of photographs will help you make a selection that's right for you.

The Surfaces

| stone | ceramic tile |
| glass | concrete | synthetics |
| wood | metal |

The rich and earthy tones of these slate wall tiles make it clear why we love stone in the bath. The floor, a laminate that looks exactly like natural wood, blends nicely.

Nothing beats stone for luxurious beauty and durability in the bath. Granite and marble are perennial favorites, and limestone and slate are fast catching up. In small doses, say on a countertop, stone blends with any decorating style. Large expanses generally produce a cool, contemporary look; but marble, favored by the Victorians, is often used today in period-style designs.

The beauty of stone derives from its grain and infinite variety of vibrant colors. Finishes vary from glossy and polished, to honed and matte, to tumbled—an aged, weathered look that has lately gained favor. Polished stone is slippery when wet. A honed or tumbled finish is safer for bathroom floors. Soapstone, which ages to a rich charcoal gray that you may remember from the counter of your high-school chemistry lab, is gaining popularity, as are slate, available in a variety of surprisingly bright shades, and creamy-beige limestone. No two pieces of stone look alike, which is part of its appeal; if you're seeking uniformity, consider engineered stone, an up-and-coming material created by binding stone chips and powders with resins. Nonporous and easy-care, engineered stone comes in a wide range of colors, including blues and yellows not found in natural materials.

The quality, durability, and even porosity of stones can vary greatly depending on where they are quarried and who is selling them. Seek out a reputable dealer and shop carefully.

RIGHT Decorative trim and fanciful furnishings dress up the expanses of rustic stone tiles in this bath.

stone

BELOW LEFT In a mostly white bath, a dark-green marble countertop and backsplash make a dramatic design statement.

BELOW CENTER The richness of this granite counter is enhanced by brass fittings. A drop-in sink adds to the streamlined look.

BELOW RIGHT A granite surround envelops this bathtub; another sweep of stone sheathes the wall above it.

ABOVE The elegant marble tiles surrounding this grand whirlpool tub are real, but the stone blocks on the wall are part of a trompe-l'oeil painting.

LEFT A modern version of a Victorian look, this bathroom floor combines ceramic and marble tiles in various sizes to form a decorative pattern.

LEFT Slate tiles sheathe this shower stall. A nifty niche for soaps and shampoos is recessed into the wall.

OPPOSITE In an interesting mix of textures, a highly polished counter offsets rough slate-tile walls.

BELOW Most natural stone comes in vivid colors as well as muted, earthy hues. The green-granite on this vanity top is a case in point.

durable stone surfacing will

how to care for natural stone

Some people like the look of a little wear and tear with their stone surfacing, but others, having spent a bundle on the stone, want it to look next to perfect. As a surface for the bath, natural stone is almost perfect—but not quite. Most stone is hard, durable, and water-resistant. But even extra-hard granite may stain if exposed to harsh chemicals or acidic substances, and it requires a periodic application of a sealant.

Marble and limestone are beautiful in the bath, but they stain and scratch easily. Be cautious with hair colorings and other chemicals, and wipe up spills right away. Use wax to protect a marble finish, and safeguard limestone with a sealant.

Protect all types of stone from gritty dirt, which dulls finishes over time, by sweeping regularly, then damp-mopping with a small amount of mild, nonacidic soap or cleaner. Too much soap will leave a film. Polished stone may benefit from a periodic application of a commercial polish to enhance luster and beef up protection, and repair kits are available for some stains and scratches.

ABOVE A ceramic-tile border adds pizzazz to this limestone floor.

BELOW Marble tiles are highlighted with a classical raised relief and trim.

beautify your bath forever

LEFT Small mosaic tiles encircle a bathtub.

RIGHT Small tiles decoratively frame a mirror.

BELOW LEFT Various shades of blue were used for this mosaic design.

BELOW RIGHT In this custom shower, a band of small terra-cotta color tiles relieve all-white walls, ceiling, and floor.

ceramic

Ceramic tile has been used to beautify bathrooms for many centuries, and it remains a good choice today. It is durable—more durable than some types of natural stone, in fact—and impervious to stains and moisture. Tile is manufactured in many sizes and shapes—from tiny hexagonal mosaics to 12-inch squares—and in a wealth of colors—neutrals and earth tones, pastels, brights, and iridescents. This dazzling variety permits personal expression with one-of-a-kind designs and configurations. Ceramic trim pieces and decorative borders can also create interesting effects and even mimic architectural detailing.

Glazed, shiny tiles work well on counters and walls but are not suitable for floors in the bath. For safety, choose a floor tile with a gritty, nonslip surface.

Ceramic tiles themselves are a snap to clean, but grout lines pose a challenge. You can keep grout

tile

sparkling by treating it with a sealer, and then cleaning it regularly with a mild bleach solution. Even easier, use colored grout.

When you shop, tell your dealer where you will use the tile, how much traffic it will get, and how long you expect it to last. An experienced dealer will help you make the right choice.

ABOVE To relieve a monochromtic scheme, a shower wall covered in moss-green tiles is punctuated with randomly placed, raised decorative inserts.

LEFT In a bath fit for a sultan, the intricately designed tile floor resembles a large carpet.

ABOVE AND RIGHT
The wall tile in this bath is ceramic with the look of natural stone, and it imparts an Old World air into the room, especially in combination with the dark marble vanity top. Designer details include a chair-rail molding and a mosaic-tile frame around the mirror.

bright idea
tiny tiles

Only 2 in. square or less, mosaic tiles allow great creativity. Here, they form a bathroom "rug," complete with border.

RIGHT Handsome non-slip tiles make a practical, safe choice for a tub platform.

BELOW RIGHT Because it comes in so many sizes and colors, ceramic tile lends itself to splashy, one-of-a-kind designs such as the bathroom floor shown here.

glazed or unglazed?

Ceramic tile is composed of clay, water, and other naturally occurring substances fired at high heat. Glazed tiles are covered with a ceramic coating that gives the tile body its color and finish. The glaze effectively repels moisture, stains, bacteria, allergens, and odors but also creates a shiny, potentially slippery surface. The higher the glaze, the less appropriate for use on floors. Glazed tiles are easy to clean, an important consideration in a room that requires daily maintenance.

Unglazed tiles look natural, rough, and rustic because they derive their texture and color from clay rather than from a colored coating. Unglazed quarry tiles, in rich beiges, browns, and rust, are typical of the look. Although unglazed tiles do sometimes appear on counters, they are most often used on floors, where their thickness and density make them especially durable and slip proof. Some unglazed tiles are stain resistant, but most require periodic sealing.

shapes and patterns

Play it safe with basic tile shapes and patterns as seen below, or create a one-of-a-kind design with a unique layout combined with accent and border tiles.

▌ **The basic floor tile** measures 12 x 12 in. with a ⅛- to ¼-in. grout joint.

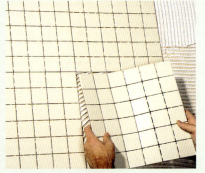

▌ **Sheet-mounted tile** will look like individual mosaic tiles when installed.

▌ **Rectangular tiles** can be used to create basket-weave patterns.

▌ **Combining different shapes** allows you to create unique patterns.

▌ **Hexagon-shaped tiles** create an interlocked pattern.

▌ **Multicolor and multisize** tiles are available in sheets.

| | | | | | trim pieces make fabulous finishing touches | | | | | | | | | |

LEFT TOP For a rich, finished look, the designer combined two types of ceramic trim in this application—a half-round molding on top and, below it, a decorative beaded border.

LEFT MIDDLE Ceramic-tile trim pieces come in an almost limitless array. This one, which is reminiscent of a classical frieze, makes an elegant transition from counter to wall.

LEFT BOTTOM This distinctive border was created by setting tan tiles at an angle against a darker green ground, then trimming the top and bottom with wood architectural moldings.

BELOW Called "subway" tiles, these classic-white 3 x 6-in. rectangles have been used in bathrooms for over a century and are popular again today.

G lass is an up-and-coming surface for sinks, countertops, walls, and even floors. Clear or colored glass sinks and counters are showing up more often, as are glass tiles. Available in many sizes and in translucent, transparent, or opaque finishes, glass tiles offer an amazing range of color—shimmering jewel-tones, frosted pastels, ambers with the look of carnival glass, and dark shades shot through with silver or gold. Large, smooth glass tiles may be too slippery for a bathroom floor, but smaller pieces with many grout lines can provide a gritty, safer surface.

Glass is durable and easy to clean, but installation is costly. If you find that a large expanse of glass tiles exceeds your budget, consider combining them with less pricey synthetics, ceramic tile, or even wood. Use the glass as a border or cover only a small area, such as a vanity top.

glass

ABOVE This design pairs cutting-edge glass with traditional marble.

Glass block, an architectural staple in the 1930s and '40s, is making a comeback in bathrooms. Because they transmit 80 percent of available natural light, these translucent blocks are ideal substitutes for windows when privacy is desired, and can also be used as shower walls or privacy partitions without compromising light or openness. Available in many square or rectangular sizes, glass block also offers several finishes and textures.

ABOVE AND BELOW In both of these bathrooms, glass block keeps the space bright, but private, whether it is used on an exterior wall (above) or an interior wall (below).

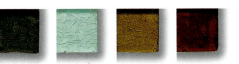

ABOVE Glass wall tiles in various shades of pale green give off a subtle but luminous glow.

ABOVE Turquoise glass tiles and white grout look crisp on a built-in vanity.

ABOVE RIGHT Blue and green glass tiles recall the colors of the ocean and guarantee a refreshing shower.

LEFT AND RIGHT Whatever their size, shape, or color, glass tiles share a luminous quality. At left, same-color grout creates a uniform look; at right, gray grout lines around irregularly shaped red tiles appear rustic and rugged.

OPPOSITE Glass tiles come in a rainbow of colors, and even the earthiest shades offer sheen and depth.

cool glass is a hot surfacing material in today's bath

LEFT For a sleek and seamless look, an integral sink is carved out of this concrete counter.

BELOW A creamy ivory color has a softening effect on concrete. The vessel lav, which looks like a bowl, adds panache.

BOTTOM AND BELOW LEFT Mixed with bits of stone or colored glass, concrete takes on a glamorous glow.

Considered daring and unconventional only a dozen years ago, concrete is now gaining wide acceptance for surfaces in the bath, as well as for tubs and showers. Surprisingly, this mundane material can be formed into graceful shapes and topped with several types of finishes—rough and rustic; glossy and polished; or subtly glowing. If you were expecting a boring, sidewalk-like surface, you'll find the color selection surprising, too. Although many homeowners prefer muted, earthy shades such as ivory, pearl gray, or sand, vivid hues are also available, depending on the skill and inventiveness of the concrete fabricator.

Treated with chemicals, pigments, and epoxy coatings—or mixed with bits of metal or colored glass—concrete also takes on the look of stone. This potential for uniqueness is part of this material's appeal.

Concrete is a natural choice, of course, for a minimalist or contemporary decorating scheme, but used in conjunction with more conventional elements, such as wood or ceramic tile, it is equally at home in a traditional-style bathroom. Concrete counters are not available off the shelf, nor is this a job for a do-it-yourselfer. To assure good results, you will need a specialist to fabricate the concrete for you. Although concrete itself is not expensive, the professional fabrication will set you back, in total, about as much as natural stone surfacing would. Still, it is important that you seek out an experienced contractor or fabricator. And before you make a decision to go with concrete, ask the fabricator to show you a counter, sink, or tub surround that has been in place for some time.

concrete

ABOVE This concrete counter looks right at home paired with traditional wood cabinets and mirrors. Like most stone, concrete has to be sealed against moisture. Even so, it may crack.

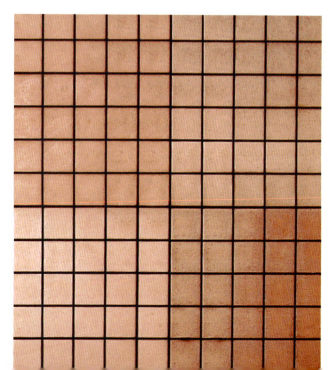

ABOVE LEFT Many looks are possible with versatile concrete. This design resembles ceramic tile with a rougher, more textured finish.

ABOVE LEFT CENTER Diamond-polished concrete tiles have the patina of matte steel. The small rectangles of aggregate have been left natural.

LEFT This sheet of concrete tile has been stained a soft terra-cotta color.

LEFT In a handsome juxtaposition of color and material, paneled-wood sheathing supports a concrete deck around a tub.

BELOW LEFT A vanity top and an elongated lav designed for two people have been seamlessly cast in concrete.

BELOW Concrete can be molded into many graceful shapes, such as this bowl sink that sits atop a concrete pedestal.

concrete facts

If you're afraid that a concrete counter or tub surround in your bathroom will resemble the floor in your garage or the sidewalk outside your house, take another look. The colors, finishes, and special effects possible with concrete are quite varied, and none of them resemble a nasty garage floor. In fact, even a simple concrete application without any bells and whistles appears sleek and streamlined.

If it is treated with a sealant, concrete will stand up well to wear and moisture, provided you wipe up spills right away, clean the surface regularly with a non-abrasive cleanser, and renew the sealant twice a year. Hairline cracks do tend to develop, but they are generally not structural and can be easily repaired. And not to worry—most experts say concrete gets more beautiful as it ages.

down-to-earth concrete creates dazzling effects

ABOVE Unlike stone, solid surfacing can be formed into a variety of shapes. This tub surround is an elegant case in point—the tub itself, the steps, the intricate edge trim, and the curvy backsplash are all made from solid surfacing.

LEFT As these tiles demonstrate, solid surfacing comes in a variety of faux-stone patterns.

RIGHT It looks like marble but this floor is actually resilient vinyl, an economical substitute for the real thing.

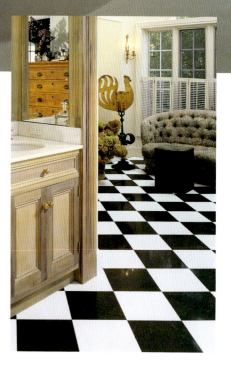

Since the 1930s, when plastic laminate first hit the marketplace, manufacturers have been hard at work creating surfacing products that resemble stone but cost less money and need less maintenance. Available in hundreds of colors, patterns, and finishes, laminates are the least costly of these synthetics, and post-formed, ready-to-install laminate countertops are even more economical. Laminate flooring mimics wood, tile, or stone and provides easy-clean durability underfoot, as does resilient vinyl flooring,

synthetics

another cost-conscious choice, which is available in a multitude of patterns. Introduced about 30 years ago, solid surfacing, a tough, color-through material made of polyesters or acrylics, can look like stone but is more malleable and can be formed into many shapes, including architectural edges and integral sinks. Composites mix quartz compounds with manmade resins to create surfaces that are nearly impervious to wear and tear. In a recent technological advance, some synthetic countertops offer an antibacterial layer that repels mold and mildew.

ABOVE Cut out to accommodate an under-mount sink, this solid-surfacing material resembles terrazzo.

RIGHT Quartz-like composite surfacing combines durability and low maintenance with the look and feel of stone.

fabulous fakes

When it comes to bathroom surfacing materials, the real thing isn't always the best thing. True, nothing beats the beauty and luxury of stone, but if your budget precludes it, why not check out solid-surfacing or composite materials? Both look almost as good as stone, most applications cost slightly less, and the materials have been engineered to resist the chemicals and acidic substances that can stain marble or granite. Because the color goes all the way through solid-surfacing material, scratches and nicks can be gently sanded away without leaving a scar, a big advantage over both high-end stone and low-cost laminate, which, once scratched, are diffi-cult to repair. Solid-surfacing material does not require any special treatment, just regular swipes with a damp cloth.

Composites, which are made of quartz particles combined with acrylic resins, duplicate the pigmentation, swirls, and veins of natural materials, particularly granite. The color range incorporates both earth tones and brights such as blue, green, red, and yellow. Also a low-maintenance product, a composite surface is extremely hard and durable, resists scratches and stains, and does not need to be sealed either for protection or to enhance its shine.

LEFT Crafted of solid-surfacing material that looks like soapstone, this vanity counter boasts an integral backsplash with a narrow ledge for toiletries.

OPPOSITE LEFT AND RIGHT Solid-surfacing materials can be successfully used with any décor. In this bath, the rich pinkish-beige of the vanity counter and tub deck blend with tradi-tional elements, such as the wood-paneled cabinets and tub surround.

RIGHT A quartz-like composite counter comes in one of about a dozen shades. The quartz particles in its composition create a subtle sheen.

stone look-alikes offer low-maintenance luxury

bright idea

on the edge

Great-looking edge treatments can dress up a basic laminate counter. Try a beveled or routed edge made of wood, metal, tile, or solid-surfacing material.

high-style on a tight budget

ABOVE Plastic laminate in a bird's-eye maple finish sheathes a curvy vanity and the medicine cabinet above it.

ABOVE RIGHT This laminate faux-wood flooring is a good choice in a bathroom or in any wet area.

RIGHT One of the great advantages of plastic laminate is the wealth of finishes available. The metal-look laminate here is the perfect surface for a contemporary-style bathroom cabinet.

laminate—a perennial favorite

Its low cost and huge range of colors, patterns, and finishes make plastic laminate a perennially popular and practical surfacing material. Laminate counters are susceptible to stains and scratches and do not last forever, but the availability of the material and the ease and economy of replacing it counteract these minor drawbacks. To minimize marks, choose a matte finish and light color, which mask signs of wear.

BELOW Covered top to bottom in a standard-issue ivory laminate, this vanity cabinet looks quite stylish, even with the edge seam showing.

Many bath surfacing materials have a rich look, but none of them can compete with the gleaming and familiar warmth of wood. Conventional wisdom has long dictated that wood and the moisture in the bath shouldn't mix, but there are ways to make it work.

Underfoot, wood is friendlier and more resilient—and warmer—than cool, hard natural stone or ceramic tile. Any wood species successfully used for flooring is appropriate for the bath provided it is installed and prepared properly. However, do keep in mind that certain woods resist moisture, and the decay that results from it, better than others, notably cedar, redwood, and teak. Narrow floor boards—2 inches wide, for example—work better in the bathroom than wide boards. The skinny strips absorb less moisture and swell and shrink slightly less than wider boards. To protect any wood floor from the effects of moisture and humidity, apply several coats of polyurethane, or try one of the new sealants called watershed protectors, all of which repel water better than an oiled or waxed finish. However, even a protected floor can be damaged by standing water, so wipe up spills right away and use a bath mat when you step out of the bathtub or shower.

Finish wood countertops with the same sealants you would use on the floor or invest in a ready-made, pretreated butcher-block counter. There is some evidence that natural substances in wood prevent the buildup of bacteria, a bonus for a bathroom countertop. Resist the impulse to cover the shower in wood—the constant exposure to water takes a serious toll, even on moisture-resistant species that have been sealed.

Vacuum or sweep wood floors and wash regularly with a barely damp mop and mild cleanser or special wood soap. Stay ahead of moisture damage by renewing protective finishes every few years and installing a ventilation system to whisk away humidity.

OPPOSITE An under-mount sink, simple lines, and the use of a light-toned wood give this vanity a contemporary flavor.

RIGHT Why shouldn't the bath look as good as any other room in the house? The graciousness of this traditional-style design is enhanced by the wood paneling, flowered wallpaper, and an ornate mirror.

BELOW In a country-style bathroom, the vanity is composed of a wood counter set atop a weathered-looking pine chest of drawers. An antique cupboard serves as a medicine cabinet.

BELOW RIGHT Bead-board wainscoting wraps around the walls and the tub in this bath.

metal

Further proof that bathroom design has come a long way from the bland box with three white fixtures is the appearance of metal as a surfacing material. Frequently used in smart-looking kitchens on appliances, and, occasionally, on countertops, metal seems an unlikely candidate for bathroom use. But it is coming on strong lately, especially in the form of tiles, and on walls as well. Although this cutting-edge material is practically indestructible, which is an advantage, it is also cold to the touch, and to the eye, which is not especially desirable. To keep this coolness from dominating, designers typically use metal sparingly, often in combination with softer, warmer materials. For example, an expanse of metal tiles might be offset by a limestone or wood floor, or intermixed with ceramic tile. For a really innovative look, try a vanity counter in copper, bronze, or brass.

Metal is an especially sanitary surface—it repels bacteria and discourages the growth of mildew. It doesn't absorb stains, won't crack, and it cleans easily. In time, all types of metal will scratch, particularly copper. To mask marks, choose a brushed, textured, or matte finish. Copper can be sealed against discoloration, or you can let it age gracefully to a burnished patina.

ABOVE TOP This metal tile boasts a lightly textured surface, one of several finishes available. Metal tiles come in various sizes, too, allowing homeowners to use them in small doses and combine them with other materials, particularly other types of tiles.

ABOVE Mixing material is an up-and-coming trend in bathroom design. In this application, large squares of subdued, earth-toned ceramic tiles are enlivened by the addition of shimmering metal insert tiles.

RIGHT Used judiciously, metal can be incorporated into any decorating style, but it is a natural for contemporary interiors. In this ultra-sleek bath, with its stone walls and floor, brushed metal forms a curve on the sculpturesque vanity.

There's tremendous variety in sinks and faucets—and even in toilets and bidets. It's wonderful having so many interesting shapes, colors, and features from which to choose, but it can also be a bit daunting. As you wade through the possibilities, keep in mind the requirements of your bathroom, including durability, performance, and easy maintenance. Fortunately, there are so many great-looking, hard-working fixtures and fittings available that you won't have to sacrifice glamour for practicality.

The Lav and Toilet

▎ lavs ▎ lav faucets ▎
▎ toilets ▎ bidets ▎

Simple wall-mounted fittings serve this artful lav. The abstract shape of the above-counter basin makes it look like a bowl set at a jaunty angle to the table top.

B athroom lavs have changed more dramatically in recent years than any other design element, taking on new and intriguing shapes, vivid colors, and unconventional materials. White, bone, and black are still big sellers, but if you want to get adventurous, there are plenty of alternatives.

When you shop, focus on your budget and the type, size, and style of your bath, lest you be seduced by a fabulous, expensive lav that won't suit your needs. For a family or master bath, where two or more people greet the day at the same time, you'll need two lavs, a roomy counter, and storage below; if space is tight, a freestanding or wall-hung model will free up floor area. Unless your bath is contemporary or eclectic in style, you may want to save exotic styles and materials for a guest bath or a powder room.

Most sinks are still made of porcelain, glazed vitreous china, or enameled cast iron—durable materials that are resistant to water, stains, and mildew. Innovative shapes and colors are possible with solid surfacing, cultured stone, concrete, metal, and glass. But stone and concrete should be sealed or they will stain, and glass and metal are susceptible to scratches.

You can expect to pay about $100 for a basic white or beige drop-in or pedestal model; for colored or integral lavs, add a couple of hundred to that. Ornate pedestal sinks or designer lavs in unusual materials or vivid colors run from $300 to about $700. For custom-made, hand-painted, and one-of-a-kind lavs, you'll have to part with $1,000 or more.

OPPOSITE LEFT This integral sink is shaped from a deep-blue solid-surfacing material with stone-like speckles.

OPPOSITE RIGHT Resurrected from Victorian times, porcelain pedestal sinks are popular in today's baths.

ABOVE LEFT Twin lavs make busy baths more efficient. Here, two drop-in basins sit in a double vanity with a tiled countertop.

ABOVE This bronze-tone basin is mounted under a wood deck.

LEFT These under-mounted lavs, made of vitreous china, maintain the smooth, elegant lines of a marble countertop.

BELOW Concrete bowls, tinted in soft, earthy hues, are designed for above-counter installation.

BELOW LEFT A rugged-looking console combines a cast-concrete integral sink with a wooden base; a shelf supplies storage.

BELOW RIGHT Pedestal sinks are ideal for small spaces; this one has sufficient decking to hold soaps and toothbrushes.

BELOW LEFT Cast-concrete vessel-style lavs are partially dropped into a cast-concrete console for an ultra-contemporary look.

BELOW RIGHT Twin pedestal lavs save space in a small master bath.

RIGHT In an opulent bath, a unique porcelain console holds two sinks fitted with gleaming brass faucets.

OPPOSITE In a masterful mix of materials, a metal base supports a shiny chrome sink set into a glass counter.

the many looks of today's pedestal and console lavs

ABOVE Select an undermount lav if you're after a streamlined look for your vanity top.

ABOVE RIGHT A concrete above-counter bowl in rich yellow looks great paired with hand-forged, highly textured fittings.

LEFT A drop-in lav is generally an economical option. This porcelain bowl looks crisp against a slate-tile countertop.

BELOW LEFT In this seamless installation, the sink and counter-top are formed from a single slab of solid-surfacing material.

RIGHT This deep rectangular lav was neatly set into a ceramic countertop by routing out a notch in the substrate.

OPPOSITE TOP A diminutive stainless-steel basin mounted under a marble surround saves floor space in a tiny Victorian-style powder room.

pros and cons of mounting styles

Before you chose a lav, decide which type of installation best satisfies your needs, budget, and design preferences.

▎**Drop-in** lavs (also called self-rimming or rimmed) are readily available, easy to install, and, provided you choose white or beige, inexpensive. Disadvantages? The rim doesn't protect countertops from splashes if the basin is shallow. Also, grime can accumulate under the outside edge.

▎**Freestanding** or wall-mounted models take up little space, making them ideal for small or accessible baths—wheelchairs slide right under some of them. The downside—plumbing is exposed, there's little or no counter area and under-counter storage is nonexistent.

▎**Undermount** lavs, which are attached to the underside of a finished counter opening, maximize deck area, look sleek,

and clean easily. However, the countertop material must be impervious to water. Standard laminate is unsuitable, and wood, unless properly sealed, will soon rot, peel, or buckle.

▎**Integral** lavs, also sleek looking and easy to clean, are low cost if made from cultured stone or concrete; solid surfacing and natural stone are pricier. The downside—most integral bowls are shallow and prone to splashing unless they are paired with low-profile faucets.

▎**Above-counter,** or vessel, lavs are stylish and trendy and require wall- or deck-mounted faucets. They can be costly and delicate depending on the material you choose; installation may be expensive, too.

today's trends

Exotic materials. Today, a lav can be made from just about any material that will hold water—stone, concrete, hand-blown or hand-painted glass, and many kinds of metal from stainless steel and copper to luxurious pewter, silver, and even gold. The newest trend is wood, a seemingly unlikely material. But, according to manufacturers, wood lavs can be pretreated and sealed to resist warping, rotting, or buckling.

Lav furniture. Chests of drawers, marble-topped wash stands, streamlined tables, fancy metal bases—all are turning up to hold lavs and act as vanities. Transform your own furniture into a one-of-a-kind piece or check manufacturers' offerings.

Color. No longer content with white or beige, homeowners are asking for—and getting—color. Co-existing with the exotic-materials trend, the color revolution has introduced vivid reds and blues, deep greens, rich earth tones, and tropical shades such as mango, tangerine, and lime to the lav palette. In addition to solid colors, painted designs are available, usually as special orders.

Shapes. Typical round and oval designs are available in all of the hot new colors and materials, of course. But you can also purchase or custom-order rectangles, squares, long troughs, bowls, and any number of free-flowing sculpturesque configurations.

pretty in pink

Today, lavs are available in every color in the rainbow, and then some. A case in point is a curvy pink sink, looking especially interesting against a black granite counter.

OPPOSITE TOP LEFT Ornate and unique, this concrete and mosaic-tile wall-mounted sink might have come out of a centuries' old castle.

OPPOSITE TOP RIGHT With their open table-like design, console-style vanities provide the illusion of space. This one contains a stainless-steel lav and boasts a handy towel bar.

LEFT Looking more like it belongs in the bedroom, this bathroom vanity features a granite top inset with a shapely pink lav.

ABOVE RIGHT A lav set into a freestanding marble and chrome vanity is a retro mid-twentieth-century design.

RIGHT This vivid green-marble bowl can be mounted on top of or underneath a counter.

ABOVE Elegant fittings in brushed bronze complement the handsome mocha-tone marble countertop in this bathroom.

RIGHT Dramatically mounted on a mirror, this antique bronze widespread faucet flows into a matching above-counter lav.

ABOVE RIGHT Polished chrome, tried, true, and durable, is enlivened here with touches of gleaming copper.

FAR RIGHT In this unusual single-hole faucet, the chrome lever emerges from a ceramic spout that looks like a miniature water pitcher.

OPPOSITE TOP RIGHT Used together, distressed-nickel faucets and a tinted concrete basin share a soft, weathered appearance.

lav faucets

Although basic, no-nonsense lav faucets are still widely available, most homeowners prefer to make a splash with more adventurous fittings and finishes. If you shop smart, you can bring home a beautiful faucet without breaking the bank.

Fortunately, you don't have to sacrifice panache for practicality: faucet function has improved along with appearance. New technologies have made possible anti-scald features, flow-rate restrictors, and motion-controlled models, and basic construction has seen improvement as well.

Faucet construction is not much fun to think about, but the outer glamour of shapes and finishes will cease to please you if the innards fail. Compression valves, an older type of construction, use washers to control water flow; this is the least expensive type of construction but also the least reliable because washers frequently wear out and need replacing. Newer, washerless types include cartridge units, which are reliable but somewhat costly to repair, and ceramic-disc valves, which are very durable and nearly maintenance free. Solid-brass or brass-and-metal innards are more reliable than plastic parts. Basic compression-valve fittings are downright cheap. If you ante up a little more for cartridge or ceramic-disc construction, you've made a smart investment. Having selected a faucet that won't need frequent repair or replacement, you can focus on sparkling finishes and alluring shapes, for which you could pay anywhere from a couple of hundred to thousands of dollars.

faucet **l**ingo

Want to be a savvy shopper? Buy a lav and faucet at the same time, matching them in style and making sure the fittings match the number of predrilled holes in the lav. Also, check that the faucet's spout reaches well into the basin.

▌ **Centerset fittings** require only one hole. They combine a spout and two handles that are set about 4 in. apart, center to center, in a single base.

▌ **Widespread fittings** require three predrilled holes. These faucets place hot- and cold-water controls 8 to 12 in. apart, center to center, with the spout generally in between them. Valves and spout appear to be separate.

▌ **Single-hole fittings** require one hole and condense the spout and control for both hot and cold water into one unit.

Any of these configurations can be **deck-** or **wall-mounted.** Deck-mounted fittings are installed into the area surrounding the basin—the rim—or the countertop. Wall-mounted fittings are installed into the wall behind the basin. In either case, the spout must be long enough to direct water into the center of the bowl.

OPPOSITE TOP LEFT This deck-mounted widespread set features an oil-rubbed bronze finish and cross handles.

▌

OPPOSITE TOP RIGHT Sized for a small sink, this centerset boasts a brushed satin finish, a graceful spout, and porcelain handle inserts.

▌

ABOVE In an ingenious and visually harmonious application, two single-hole fittings service a long rectangular integral sink.

▌

LEFT Clean-lined faucets with an architectural look are just right with a square undermount lav.

▌

RIGHT Brushed-nickel, wall-mounted fittings offer a modern version of classic cross-handle styling.

LEFT Wave your hands under this wall-mounted, motion-controlled spout, and water will flow. Its rustic copper finish is in keeping with the concrete bowl and rugged counter.

ABOVE A brushed-satin brass finish dresses up this widespread set that has an arc spout and easy-to-use lever handles.

BELOW Ornate metalwork gives these solid-brass fittings an antique appearance.

finding the right finish

As you shop for faucets you will find that fancy finishes flourish. Chrome, an old standby, is durable, affordable, tarnish resistant, and always looks good. But if you don't mind a little extra expense and upkeep, you can add big sparkle to your bath with brass, nickel, bronze, colored baked-on epoxy porcelain, stainless steel—even gold, silver, or platinum. On polished finishes, water spots and scratches stand out, requiring more care and polishing than brushed, satin, or matte treatments. Most finishes show wear over time, especially if you use abrasive cleansers. A relatively new development, a physical vapor deposition (PVD) finish, increases costs by about 30 percent but promises a lasting shine.

ABOVE Period-style details on this deck-mounted "bridge" design include a lustrous brushed-copper finish, gooseneck spout, and traditional cross handles.

BELOW The rustic, aged look of these hand-forged stainless steel and brass fixtures would be at home in a country-style bath or a contemporary one.

TOP A layered design articulated in gold and silver has an unusual and architectural look; water ripples as it flows through the open spout.

ABOVE Sleek polished-chrome fittings mounted onto the wall are designed to direct water into an above-counter lav.

As the bathroom settles into the twenty-first century, the toilet is keeping up with major technological advances. In recent years, new introductions have included heated seats, hydraulically operated seats that move up and down for greater accessibility, low-flow toilets, and now dual-flush toilets that offer a specialized flushing system—a half flush for liquids or a full flush for solids. These models save about 30 percent more water than low-flush ones. Innovations aside, there are still only a couple of basic types for your choosing.

Most toilets have two pieces, a tank and bowl that are bolted together at installation. Higher-priced one-piece toilets usually come with a seat; two-piece units do not. With one-piece construction, there are no crevices between the bowl and tank to

toilets

leak or collect dirt, and the flush is much quieter. Concealed tanks, installed between wall studs behind the toilet bowl, are also available.

You also have the choice of either a round or an elongated bowl. Round bowls are the most common, least expensive, and the most practical for tight spaces. Elongated bowls have a sleeker look and offer extra room in front, but they cost more.

Most toilets are made from white vitreous china, which provides a durable, stain-resistant, and cleanable surface. Colors are available, as are different shapes—sculptural and modern or classic and architectural. Low-profile models are streamlined, and traditional tall-tank toilets look stylish in stainless steel or with hand-painted details. Reproductions of Victorian toilets with wall-mounted tanks and pull chains remain popular for homeowners with period-style baths.

A basic two-piece white toilet costs about $100. Add color, designer styling, or special features and the price can go up by several hundreds or even thousands of dollars.

ABOVE AND LEFT Classic "architectural" molded features unite the toilet, tub, and pedestal sink in an ensemble of bath fixtures. This ergonomic toilet is built to universal height, making it easy for users to move from a sitting to standing position.

ABOVE RIGHT In a modern rendition of a classic, a two-piece toilet with a wood seat is paired appropriately with a vintage-looking pedestal sink to give this powder room period charm.

RIGHT Once reserved for institutional use, stainless steel is an emerging trend in residential baths. Here, leather—another unconventional but increasingly popular material for the bathroom—covers the front of the toilet tank and the face of the vanity cabinet.

ABOVE LEFT A one-piece toilet with an elongated bowl presents a sleek low profile.

ABOVE A curved tank and a bowl that looks as if it is sitting on a pedestal base distinguishes this two-piece model.

LEFT A one-piece low-profile toilet fits neatly under an extended counter.

OPPOSITE TOP AND BOTTOM Fixtures can enhance your design. Witness the spare lines of this contemporary matching suite.

gravity or pressure

Another choice faces you when you go shopping—will you use gravity or pressure to flush your new toilet?

Gravity-flush toilets are the familiar kind—water from the tank flushes the bowl clean. In the old days, when as much as 7 gal. of water created a powerful flush, they worked fine. But because today's toilets are restricted to 1.6 gal. or less per flush, more than one flush may be necessary to clear the bowl.

Pressure-assist toilets rely on water pressure in the line to compress air, which then works with a small amount of water to blast the bowl clean. This method produces a more efficient flush and uses less water. Pressure-assisted toilets are more expensive than gravity-fed models, more difficult to repair, and noisier when they're flushed.

ABOVE Copper trim on the toilet tank is designed to coordinate the fixture with the undermount copper basin in the lav console.

TOP This ultra-chic toilet boasts a two-piece copper body and a wooden seat.

LEFT A French-imported two-piece toilet with hand-painted flowers and decorative trim is almost too pretty to use.

in today's bath even the toilet can be gorgeous

LEFT AND BELOW LEFT With unusual materials and clean-lined design, either of these toilets would look smashing in a modern bathroom. One toilet is completely stainless steel; the other combines stainless steel with a cherry tank panel and seat.

BELOW Based on a nineteenth-century French design, this solid-ash toilet throne features arm rests and hand-painting on the vitreous china flush cistern, the ceramic plaque, and the chain pull.

fashionable or functional, attention to details

will make a difference ||||||||||||||||||||||||||||||||||||||||||||||||

OPPOSITE ABOVE With a gentle push, this chip-resistant polypropylene toilet seat closes slowly and quietly.

ABOVE AND INSET A graceful two-piece toilet is equipped with a quiet-close seat that lifts off easily, allowing access to usually hard-to-clean areas. The seat's high-gloss finish blends seamlessly with the toilet's vitreous china body.

LEFT AND OPPOSITE BOT-TOM LEFT AND RIGHT Toilet handles come in new styles and materials. Choosing one that blends with the other elements in your bath will help pull the whole design together.

bidets

Bidets are fixtures for personal hygiene that came to the United States from France a couple of decades ago and have slowly but steadily grown in popularity since then. Originally designed in the eighteenth century for personal hygiene between weekly baths, bidets closely resemble toilets, but require more complicated plumbing and cost more.

Some bidets are fitted with a faucet that fills the bowl, the same way a sink is filled. In other models a vertical or horizontal spray issues a gentle shower of water, while still other units offer both of those options. Some newer fixtures combine the functions of a toilet and a bidet in one unit.

Bidets require a hot-and-cold supply line, a drain, and about 8 square feet of space. They are produced by all major manufacturers in the same colors and styles as other bathroom fixtures, whether traditional or contemporary. Prices range from about $300 to perhaps $1,000 for colors or special finishes, such as stainless steel.

Brass

Chrome

Brass and Chrome

Oil-Rubbed Bronze

Brushed Nickel

ABOVE LEFT Inspired by the shape of an egg, this avant-garde suite of fixtures includes a tub, an above-counter lav, and a wall-hung, spray-style bidet. The toilet is behind the sliding frosted-glass partition.

ABOVE In a coordinated bath design, even the hinges on the toilet seat can be an eyesore if they clash with other elements. One of these hinges is sure to match your faucets and other hardware.

ABOVE RIGHT AND RIGHT A technologically advanced low-profile toilet does double duty as a bidet, incorporating a warm-water personal-cleansing system with its own handy control panel. The toilet also boasts dual-flush capability and an easy-to-clean concave rim.

5

What is one of the blessings of bigger bathrooms? There's finally room for plentiful storage—and so many efficient and interesting ways to supply it. The tried-and-true vanity is still around, but there are also storage pieces that mimic antiques and bathroom "furniture" that provides places for absolutely everything. Even medicine cabinets have evolved into important design elements. For inspiration, study the photographs on the following pages where you'll find the latest looks. You can also read up on the trends and improvements that can organize your bathroom and make your life easier.

Vanities and Storage

❙ vanities ❙ cabinet construction ❙
❙ define your style ❙ cabinet finishes ❙
❙ bathroom furniture ❙ medicine
cabinets ❙

Typical of the good-looking and generously sized bathroom vanity of today, this master bath cabinet offers an abundance of drawer and behind-door storage.

The design attention that has been focused on the bathroom for several decades has improved every aspect of it. The vanity still reigns as the major supplier of storage, but these days it looks better, stores more, and has grown taller. Because one height does not suit all people, stock vanities now range from the standard 30 inches to 36 inches high, which is easier on the back for tall people. With two vanities in the master bath, each one can be tailored to a comfortable height for its user. Vanities are also available in a couple of depths these days—18-inch-deep units free up floor space; 24-inch-deep models store more. To further improve the storage picture, the vanity is often supplemented by additional cabinets, open shelves, and freestanding furniture. Even the medicine cabinet has increased in size, functionality, and good looks.

Learn some cabinet lingo before you go shopping. For example, stock vanity cabinets, your least-expensive option, are preassembled, factory-made units that you can often take home the same day. Some of them are well made and attractive, but sizes, styles, and

vanities

finishes are limited. You'll pay a little more for a semicustom design because the variety of finishes and styles is greater, but these units are also factory made and available only in standard sizes. Custom cabinets, the most pricey option, offer the greatest design leeway because they are built to your specifications.

Available at home centers and large retail stores, stock cabinets can be inexpensive, as low as about $100 for a 36-inch-wide model. Check construction carefully before you buy—not all of them are well made. A 36-inch-wide semicustom vanity, generally available through cabinet showrooms, will cost about $300. Custom units, which are available through some manufacturers or local cabinetmakers, can be costly, but you will get a well-made product that meets specific needs.

OPPOSITE This design-savvy console is available as a stock cabinet.

ABOVE A semicustom piece features a fine finish and ornate detailing.

LEFT AND RIGHT These custom vanities, equipped with several types of storage, were designed to meet the exact needs of the owners.

today's vanities let you stow your stuff in style

vanity and **c**abinet **d**imensions

STOCK BATHROOM CABINET DIMENSIONS (based on standard sizes in inches)

Cabinet	Width	Height	Depth
Sink base	15-72	28-36	16-21
Drawer base	12–21	31½-34½	21-24
Tall linen cabinet	9-24	83-96	21
Vanity linen cabinet	9-18	48-83	21
Vanity hamper cabinet	15-18	31½-33½	21

ABOVE This single custom vanity is attached to a bank of floor-to-ceiling cabinets.

ABOVE RIGHT A triple-vanity offers two sink areas and a grooming center.

RIGHT Rounded in front, this compact stock vanity provides visual interest, a little more interior storage than a flat-panel unit, and extra countertop space.

OPPOSITE TOP A tall door cabinet and a drawer unit supplement the storage offered by two vanities.

OPPOSITE BELOW To create visual interest in this contemporary bath, the designer specified frosted-green glass doors for a custom-made vanity.

bright idea

sassy glass

Frosted glass doors look slick and lighten the appearance of a large vanity cabinet. They also camouflage unsightly things, such as plumbing, cleaning products, and grooming supplies and appliances.

ABOVE Many stock vanity cabinets have the sleek good looks and architectural appeal of more expensive units.

BELOW LEFT Outfitting handsome furniture as a vanity is becoming an important bathroom trend.

BELOW RIGHT Fine-furniture detailing such as rope molding, a two-tone finish, and decorative hardware enlivens this vanity.

cabinet construction

This is the day of the discount when it comes to home-improvement products. The rock-bottom prices you see advertised sometimes may be tempting, but protect yourself from vanity "lemons" by checking cabinet quality carefully before you buy. Beware of drawers that fail to open smoothly and are held together with nails, glue, or staples. Look for interiors that are finished, including rear surfaces. If there are shelves in the vanities you like, be sure they are adjustable—another sign of quality—and that they measure ⅝-inch thick to prevent bowing. Fine solid-wood cabinets and sturdy plywood cases with solid-wood doors will withstand daily wear and tear and damage from the bathroom's moist, steamy environment. However, particleboard or laminates over particleboard do not stand up as well and may quickly warp, peel, or cup when exposed to a great deal of moisture. For help selecting a vanity countertop material, refer to Chapter 3, "The Surfaces," beginning on page 56.

BELOW LEFT It's the perfect look for a traditional bath—a vanity that resembles a wash stand, a vessel-style sink atop it, and a matching armoire for supplemental storage.

BELOW RIGHT Corner units are very handy in some bath layouts, allowing you to make the best use of space. Here, the vanity is part of a suite of cabinetry.

LEFT Glazed and slightly distressed to look like an antique chest of drawers, this vanity has roomy counter space, eight side drawers that are sized right for sundries, and storage underneath.

ABOVE For this bath the designer transformed an antique metalwork table into a one-of-a kind vanity with a granite countertop and an under-mounted sink.

furniture-style vanities

A couple of years ago somebody—an enterprising home-owner, perhaps, or an imaginative interior designer—came upon the idea of converting an antique washstand into a bath-room vanity, complete with a sink and all the necessary plumbing. The idea spread quickly, as most good ideas do, and soon many homeowners were asking their designers and remodeling contractors to help them duplicate this look. These furniture-like vanities not only added eccentric charm and relieved the monotony of banks of cabinets that all looked alike but actually provided more storage in some cases. It wasn't long before cabinet manufacturers jumped on the band-wagon and began infusing their bath collections with trendy new vanities crafted, glazed, distressed, and ornamented with classic architectural trim to look like antique wash stands, chests of drawers, and tables. Taking the idea a little bit fur-ther, cabinet companies have now added armoires, mirrors, wall cabinets, shelves, and other storage pieces and designed them to harmonize with their furniture-like vanities. The bath-room furniture trend began with antiques, but now that it has taken hold so firmly, contemporary-looking pieces—stream-lined console tables, sleek bureaus—are also available for homeowners with a preference for modern design.

framed versus **f**rameless **d**esigns

In framed construction, a rectangular frame outlines the cabinet box to add strength and provide a place to attach the door. The doors on frameless cabinets are laid flush over the box. No frame is visible, and hinges are often invisible as well.

Frameless A European concept that took hold here in the 1960s, frameless cabinets are a standby in contemporary-style bathrooms. The doors fit over the entire cabinet box for a sleek and streamlined look.

Framed Cabinets with a visible frame offer richness of detail that is appropriate for traditional and country-style bathrooms and their many design cousins.

The rooms of your home display a certain style, one that reflects your tastes and personality. Why should the bathroom be any different? No longer a bland and lackluster room, it's as valid a place as any to express your decorating sensibility. And the best place to start is with the vanity and other cabinets. They will establish the overall style, which you can reinforce with fixtures, fittings, surfaces, and accessories.

Is a casual country look your cup of tea? You might begin with pine cabinets in a light stain or a slightly distressed, painted finish. White-painted, bead board cabinets also impart a country flavor. A traditionally styled bathroom would look slightly more formal. For the vanity, you might choose rich medium- or dark-toned wood enlivened with brass hardware and some fine-furniture details, such as raised panels, rope trim, or applied molding. To create a contemporary bath you'd select clean-lined cabinets finished in laminate, metal, or light-toned woods, such as ash or birch, with minimal hardware. For a period-style, such as a Victorian bath, dark, ornately carved wood is one way to go; a lighter Victorian look would feature a white painted wood cabinet with simple detailing and a marble top. To help you achieve your design dreams, cabinet manufacturers sell all of the vanities described here and more, but you can also create a one-of-a-kind look by converting a piece of furniture or going the custom route.

define your style

OPPOSITE TOP
Custom-made bead-board vanities in a light finish establish a relaxed country look in this bath.

OPPOSITE BOTTOM
A console vanity with a concrete top creates a cool contemporary look.

BELOW LEFT
Traditionally styled and custom-made to fit a window wall, twin lavs flank a storage cabinet.

RIGHT Pale wood, clean lines, and stainless-steel door and drawer pulls make this vanity a good choice for a modern-design room.

cabinet door style choices

Door styles are strictly decorative. Styles pictured, left to right: reveal-overlay panel; frame and panel; flat panel; beaded frame and panel; square raised panel; curved raised panel; bead-board panel; and cathedral panel

bath storage has never been more appealing and

BELOW An above-counter lav sits atop a crisp, clean-lined vanity with the look of a chest of drawers.

RIGHT Point-of-use storage between two vanities holds soaps, toothbrushes, and other sundries.

BELOW RIGHT A great setup for a master bath consists of two vanities, lots of storage, and a makeup table.

OPPOSITE A vanity that resembles a nineteenth-century chest is just right for a Victorian-style bath.

tailored to individual needs

bright idea

highs and lows

New vanity sizes
accommodate people
of different heights—
no more deep bending
to wash your
face.

cabinet finishes

When it comes to finishes for vanities and other bath cabinets, richness is in, starkness is out. According to interior designers and other bath specialists, there is a strong movement nowadays toward comfort in the bath, both physical and visual. Our sybaritic bathtubs and showers pamper our bodies. Now it seems, we also want pampering for our souls with a cozy, comfortable ambiance not usually associated with the bathroom.

The desire for richness and visual comfort has led to a resurgence of wood for vanities and other bath furniture, particularly warm and mellow woods such as maple, cherry, and mahogany. Glazed finishes are also on the upswing and are being used in two ways—one, as a clear coating to add depth to natural wood finishes; secondly, to create a worn yet elegant antique patina on other pieces. This new design direction also emphasizes richer, softer color. Stark white is on its way out, being replaced by warmer whites and painted finishes and laminates in off-whites such as biscuit, very pale yellows, and delicate pastels.

OPPOSITE Opulent detailing and the use of two different wood stains—one dark, one light—distinguish this vanity.

ABOVE LEFT Painted finishes in pastels and creamy hues, such as this pale buttery yellow, are making a comeback.

ABOVE Antiqued and glazed, this high-style vanity has the well-worn charm of your grandmother's bedroom furniture.

LEFT Economical and easy-to-clean, decorative laminate has been a favorite cabinet finishing material for many years.

ABOVE The look of fine old furniture characterizes this new bath cabinetry. A dark stain, marble counters, and porcelain hardware envelop the room in richness.

RIGHT With its warm wood cabinetry, brass hardware, and oversized mirror leaning against the wall, this bathroom has the aura of a gentleman's dressing room in an English manor house.

bathroom furniture

Furniture-like vanities have been such a big hit with homeowners that they have given rise to another trend—bathroom "furniture." Now, instead of restricting themselves to a single, unique-looking vanity that resembles a piece of furniture, designers are outfitting baths with several freestanding pieces, all of which look like they have been imported from the bedroom, living room, or even the kitchen. Because new bathrooms, especially master baths, tend to be large today, they can accommodate similarly scaled pieces such as bureaus, sideboards, and armoires. Besides, furniture introduces a degree of warmth and coziness not typically found in the bathroom. You can implement the look in your own bath by importing pieces from other rooms in your house or by scouring flea markets and antique stores to find a few likely candidates. If those shopping jaunts seem like too much of an effort, you can turn to cabinet manufacturers, many of whom have recently introduced custom-made, furniture-quality bath cabinets into their lines. And you'll be glad to know that this new design approach has done more than beautify the bathroom—it has also improved storage capacity. A 6-foot-tall armoire will look fabulous and will hold more items than a standard cabinet; as will the new bureau-like vanities, with their drawers of various sizes and shapes.

BELOW Frosted-glass cabinet doors, a trendy addition to bath cabinetry, enhance the mellowness of this antique finish.

RIGHT Armoires provide attractive and functional storage. Keep the contents neatly arranged and leave one door ajar for a pretty display.

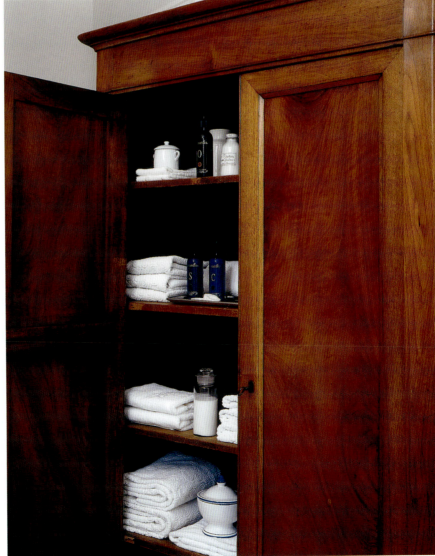

matching "suites"

OPPOSITE TOP Designed to be used together, these three pieces display different details and two finishes for an informal and lively look.

OPPOSITE BOTTOM A cherry stain and architectural detailing beautify a roomy bureau-like vanity. The matching tall cabinet is for towels.

RIGHT A cherry glaze, bead detailing on the drawer and door fronts, and abundant compartments distinguish this group of cabinets.

BELOW Soft, mossy green, a new color for the bath, looks great with porcelain hardware and glass-fronted wall units.

bright idea

how suite it is

Taking its cue from the kitchen, this cabinet ensemble maximizes storage for the bath with drawers and cupboards in handy sizes.

open shelving

In the bathroom, you don't have to stow all your stuff behind closed doors. In fact, it's convenient to have some items, such as towels and soaps, up for grabs when you need them. That's where open shelves come in handy. They're economical, practical, and, if used imaginatively to show off pretty perfume bottles, graceful jars of lotions, or stacks of colorful towels, they can be decorative, too.

The flexibility of open shelves lets you use every square inch of the bath to create new storage, including places that a standard cabinet won't fit. For example, convert the space between wall studs into shallow sets of shelves for toiletries and small bottles. Nooks such as these can be created anywhere in the room, but they are particularly handy near the sink. Install a couple of shelves above the tub for extra towels. To compensate for the lack of a vanity, put a little shelf above a pedestal sink. Go to it—the possibilities are practically endless.

LEFT AND ABOVE RIGHT Making clever use of the space between wall studs, the designer of this bath created shelves on both sides of the vanity. One keeps towels handy; the other holds a TV and linen-covered storage boxes.

RIGHT In this master bath, a tall cabinet placed between his-and-her sinks stores soaps and lotions at the point of use—and keeps them off the countertop.

LEFT Carved out of an otherwise unusable space between the vanity and bedroom door, tall, narrow shelves store towels and display collectibles.

BELOW Adjustable glass shelves set into a niche near a makeup center holds cosmetics and perfumes.

BELOW LEFT Wasted space above the tub next to the shower is put to use with shelves for towels.

organizers keep your stuff from straying

ABOVE Keep cosmetics of all sizes beautifully neat and easy to find with a clever divided drawer.

LEFT A wire bin on the inside of a cabinet door is a perfect place for a hair dryer, a curling iron, and their pesky cords.

ABOVE RIGHT This cupboard in a vanity cabinet features a pullout shelf for items that get used every day.

RIGHT Just the right size for shampoos, conditioners, and other tall bottles, this shelf attaches to the inside of a cabinet door.

OPPOSITE A handy compartmentalized drawer such as this one comes as standard equipment with many stock cabinets.

how much is enough?

Storage is a problem in every room of the house, partly because many people don't plan ahead for what they need and partly because they let "stuff" accumulate. In the bath, the problem is especially acute. For one thing, this room may be the smallest space in the house. For another, most people have become accustomed to insufficient storage, making do with the limited space under a standard vanity or a few wobbly shelves. Fortunately, you don't need to settle anymore— bath storage has never been better. Still as you plan your new or remodeled bath, it's a good idea to figure out as closely as possible how much storage you will need to maintain neatness, organization, and serenity.

Here's one way to do it: empty every drawer, cupboard, and shelf in your existing bath into a couple of cartons (you may need more than a couple), and don't forget to include whatever is on the countertops. Sort through it all, throwing out ratty towels, expired medicines, old makeup, flattened tubes of toothpaste, and anything else that is not a bathroom necessity. While you're at it, check the bedroom—are there any items in there that you would prefer to store in the bath but haven't had the room? Once you're down to everything you want handy in the bathroom, divide the items into categories—toiletries, medicines, bath linens, grooming aids, cleaning supplies, hot-water bottles, heating pads, and so forth. If you look over the categories carefully, you'll be able to estimate pretty closely how much and what kind of storage you'll need to keep everything convenient and in its proper place. And here's a bonus: you'll have purged your bathroom of years of accumulated junk.

OPPOSITE TOP Honey-toned cabinets and a striking marble countertop create elegant good looks in this master bath. Underneath the glamour is a smart storage system.

OPPOSITE BOTTOM A roomy cupboard sports ribbed-glass doors.

LEFT This low-to-the-floor cabinet is placed right next to the tub so that someone taking a bath can easily grab one of the towels stacked on top. The cabinet's deep drawer can hold a pile of extra towels.

ABOVE Putting every inch of space to work for storage, easy-access niches and cubbyholes next to the sink contain items that the lady of the house uses every day.

LEFT To open up space in a small master bath, the owners installed two freestanding sinks. A built-in ledge behind the sinks and a cabinet between them compensate for a lack of under-sink storage.

RIGHT Combining wood cabinets in two different stains and styles adds visual appeal to this bathroom. With two compartments for towels and a series of small drawers, the freestanding chest is a helpful addition.

BELOW A supplemental storage cabinet in this bath has the look of an old-time filing cabinet.

top-drawer storage ideas

medicine

Medicine cabinets have been standard bathroom equipment since plumbing first came indoors. Until recently they have not been particularly efficient, but many have now evolved from little mirrored boxes to good-sized storage compartments with wide expanses of mirror. Up-to-date models also offer such features as integrated lighting, double doors with mirrors on both sides, interior cubbyholes and racks for toothbrushes and other items, deeper interiors for storing bulky items, built-in electrical outlets, and even defoggers for the mirrors. Some reproduction models have grown to include more storage area, but even small ones make impressive design statements.

OPPOSITE TOP Two ultrasleek glass vanities mounted against squares of mirror look perfect paired with mirrored, frameless medicine cabinets.

OPPOSITE BOTTOM Old medicine cabinets may not be highly efficient, but they are just the thing for a vintage-inspired or restored bathroom.

LEFT A wood-framed cabinet has a warm, classic look that's very popular today. The cabinet door is also mirrored to brighten the space.

BELOW A recessed model features adjustable shelves, an easy-clean interior, and two integral make-up lights.

cabinets

Recessed medicine cabinets are set several inches into the wall between studs. They present a streamlined appearance that harmonizes well with contemporary designs and supply a bit more interior space than wall-hung, or flush-mounted cabinets, but are more difficult to install.

By the way, in a household that includes small children, the medicine cabinet is not a good place for prescriptions. Instead, store them in a locked cabinet or drawer or in a tall cabinet where little hands can't reach them.

OPPOSITE Installing an extralong recessed cabinet involves spanning several wall studs.

ABOVE This surface-mounted installation includes numerous cabinets.

RIGHT A mirrored medicine cabinet is tucked into the wall above the electrical outlet.

removing studs for a recessed cabinet

bright idea

safety locks

Curious children are often intrigued by the contents of medicine cabinets. To prevent mishaps, you might want to invest in a model that includes a safety lock.

Determine which studs need to be removed (here, just one). Cut through individual studs using a backsaw or reciprocating saw.

Cut the header and sill pieces to finish the opening. Face-nail the header and sill to the cut studs, and toenail them to the uncut ones at the side. Place the cabinet in the opening.

In today's bigger, more beautiful baths, lighting is more important than ever. For the small unimaginative bathrooms of days gone by, a ceiling light and maybe a fixture over the sink were enough to do the job. But today, bath designers and other experts recommend a layered approach to lighting. Start with some daylight via windows or skylights that open to provide ventilation as well as light. Then add a dose of pleasant artificial light that enhances the sunshine and illuminates the whole room at night. Don't forget: you'll need task lights for efficiency and safety in bathing and grooming areas.

Light and Air

I natural light I artificial lighting I
I ventilation I

By day, cheerful sunshine streams in through the windows in this bath. At night, a pretty fixture supplies task lighting, which is reflected and magnified by the mirror.

natural light

Remodeling a bathroom often includes removing the small original windows and opening up the space with larger windows. Or you can add a skylight to flood the area with natural light without worrying about privacy issues or using up valuable wall space in a small room.

Whether you are remodeling an old bath or building a new one, pay attention to the variety of options you have for incorporating windows. You will want to get one that looks best with the rest of the room, of course, but don't forget to consider energy efficiency. Today's windows and skylights are better sealed than those produced in the past. Construction is tighter, so there is reduced air infiltration around the frames. Multiple panes, improved coatings, and gas-filled spaces between panes can reduce both heat loss and unwanted heat gain. Some coatings filter out ultraviolet rays. When shopping, always consider your climate and the window's orientation.

ABOVE A round-top window provides light and views for someone relaxing in this whirlpool bathtub.

LEFT Shutters close for privacy but still let in some daylight and fresh air.

OPPOSITE In this bath, where privacy needs precluded conventional windows, a roof window solves the problem and ushers in bountiful daylight and air.

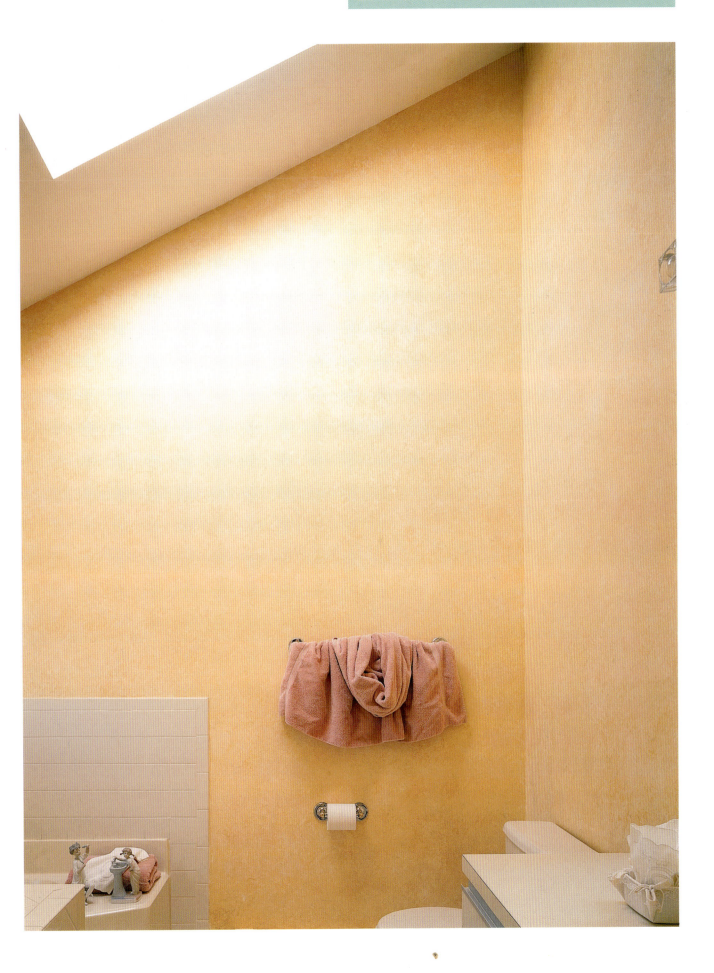

window types

Windows can be fixed (meaning you can't open them) or operable. Glass block is an example of a fixed window, but even clear-glass framed panels can be fixed. These windows let in light and views, but they don't admit air. Examples of operable window types include double- and single-hung windows.

▌ **Double-hung windows** have both an upper and lower sash that ride up and down in their own channels.

▌ **Single-hung windows** are like double-hung units except that only their lower sash moves.

▌ **Casement windows** are hinged vertically to swing in or out. You can operate them with a crank.

▌ **Sliding windows** have top and bottom tracks on which the sash move sideways.

▌ **Awning windows** are hinged horizontally to swing in or out.

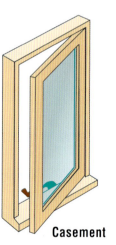

Fixed

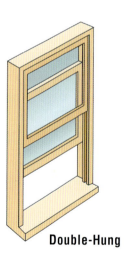

Casement

Double-Hung

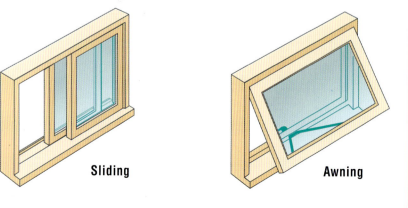

Sliding   **Awning**

LEFT An awning-style window tilts out to let hot, steamy air escape.

BELOW LEFT An expanse of glass block is a stylish way to provide both day-light and privacy.

RIGHT Old-time double-hung windows are now available fitted with energy-efficient glass.

BELOW RIGHT In this bath, casement windows frame views of a sunny deck and garden.

ABOVE In a sumptuous bathroom, an extra-large skylight is positioned over the tub, offering the opportunity for a sun-splashed—or moonlit—soak.

LEFT Operable roof windows in a tub alcove bring in an infusion of light and fresh air; after a bath, they also release warm, steamy air.

OPPOSITE LEFT A skylight channels sunshine onto deep-toned walls of stone in this bathroom, creating a warm glow.

OPPOSITE RIGHT A solar tunnel supplements the natural light provided by a roomy windowed bay.

skylights and roof windows

If you don't have access to a window, investigate a vented skylight or a roof window. Many come with electrically operated controls for easy handling. In a house with an attic, you can even install a shaft or tunnel that makes it possible to bring light and air from an operable skylight or roof window into a bathroom. Some of these units work by remote control for easy operation.

bright idea

solar tunnel

A solar tunnel lets you enjoy the benefits of a skylight without installing a standard-size skylight shaft.

artificial lighting

Good lighting provides adequate illumination and enhances the look and feeling of the space it brightens. It also increases safety. There are several types of artificial lighting. It's wise to include all of them in your plans for a new bath. The first, *ambient lighting,* is the general illumination that is required for any room. The optimum number and location of general light sources (fixtures) depends upon the size of the room. The second type, *task lighting,* is what you need for grooming. To look good in the mirror, task lighting should come at you from both sides, radiating from the middle of your face (about 60 to 66 inches from the floor for most adults). Avoid lighting the vanity area from above, which will cause shadows. The third type, *accent lighting,* isn't necessary in a bathroom, but it can add a decorative touch. Small strip lights or compact spotlights mounted inside a glass-door cabinet, under the mirror, beneath a raised tub, or recessed into a soffit above the vanity are excellent examples. They don't give off a lot of light, just enough to create a mood.

RIGHT Accent lights and mirrors expand visual space and rev up glamour in this ultracontemporary bathroom.

OPPOSITE TOP Fixtures flanking a mirror are good sources of task lighting; daylight shining through the window adds to the glow.

OPPOSITE BOTTOM The brightness provided by two period-style fixtures is sufficient for both task and ambient lighting in this grooming area.

LEFT Unobtrusive recessed ceiling fixtures deliver adequate illumination without compromising the sleek simplicity of this bathroom design.

how much do you need?

In all but the tiniest of bathrooms, ceiling-mounted lamps are necessary for sufficient general illumination. A good choice is recessed lighting. How much you need, of course, depends on the size of the room. If the bathroom is less than 100 sq. ft., one fixture is sufficient. Add another fixture for each additional 50 sq. ft. If the surfaces around the room are light-absorbing dark hues, such as mahogany-stained cabinets, deep-colored walls, or black granite countertops, you may have to compensate with stronger lamps. If the bulbs you are using are not providing enough general light, you need to substitute them with ones that have more *lumens* not with higher-wattage bulbs. The next time you shop for bulbs, read the packaging, which indicates the lumens per watt (LPW) produced by a bulb.

bright idea

dimmers

Install dimmers on the lights so that all members of the household can adjust light levels to meet their own needs.

OPPOSITE A three-lamp vintage-style wall fixture produces plenty of light power for a diminutive powder room.

ABOVE LEFT Ornate chandeliers combine with recessed ceiling lights to illuminate an opulently furnished master bath.

BELOW LEFT A room with lots of glass and other light-reflecting surfaces requires less artificial light than a room full of dark, light-absorbing surfaces.

BELOW Simple strip lighting suits a streamlined style.

LEFT Four separate fixtures mounted above a vanity mirror spread light over the large area.

BELOW LEFT AND RIGHT In these two grooming areas, fixtures are placed on either side of the mirror, which, according to lighting experts, is the best way to illuminate the face for applying makeup and shaving.

OPPOSITE TOP Two vertical lighting strips contribute to the clean-lined look of this design.

OPPOSITE BELOW Fixtures, such as individual sconces grouped above a mirror, can be used for decorative impact as well as illumination.

lighting for mirrors

You'll need even, shadow-free lighting for applying makeup, shaving, or caring for hair. It should illuminate both sides of the face, under the chin, and the top of the head. Plan to use at least 120 incandescent watts. Never aim lighting into the mirror. Decorative sconces installed on either side of a small mirror at face height do the job nicely. Place them no higher than 60 in. above the floor and at least 28 in. but not more than 60 in. apart, unless you pair them with another vanity light source.

If fluorescent side lights are mandated by your local code, use the deluxe warm-white fluorescent bulbs that more closely resemble natural light. Install them up to 48 in. apart for sufficient lighting and supplement them with recessed or surface-mounted ceiling fixtures. A large mirror used over a double vanity will require a different approach: treat each lav as a separate task area and light each one.

lighting for tubs and showers

Light around the tub and shower area has to be bright enough for safety and grooming, adjusting water temperature or showerheads, and reading (if you care to read while you soak). Recessed downlights or any other fixtures designed for wet areas are fine. Shielded fixtures eliminate glare, and shatter-resistant white acrylic diffusers are the safest. Any light fixture installed in a wet or damp area has to be protected properly so that water cannot accumulate in wiring compartments, lamp holders, or other electrical parts. Your professional electrician will know how to handle the situation and can recommend the proper fixture.

LEFT Stylish and unique, a lacy wrought-iron chandelier brightens a bathtub alcove.

RIGHT For safety, shower stalls must be well-lit. Ask your electrician about the waterproof fixtures that meet the code in your area.

BELOW A shower enclosure receives daylight through a group of windows; at night, it's lit by a recessed fixture.

OPPOSITE In a windowless tub alcove, create your own view with a pretty painting and a sunny glow from a pendant lamp.

ABOVE LEFT Low-voltage halogen bulbs in a clean-lined fixture emit a clear white light

LEFT In this bath, incandescent bulbs provide both general and task lighting.

types of bulbs

Here's a description of the most common types of bulbs and their advantages and disadvantages.

❘ Incandescent. Like sunlight, incandescent bulbs emit "continuous-spectrum light," or light that contains every color. Illumination from these bulbs, in fact, is even warmer than sunlight, making its effect very appealing in a room. It makes our skin tones look good and even enhances our feeling of well-being. The drawbacks to incandescent bulbs are that they use a lot of electricity and produce a lot of heat. However, they come in a variety of shapes, sizes, and applications. (One type features a waterproof lens cover that makes it suitable for over a tub or inside of a shower.) These bulbs can be clear, diffuse, tinted, or colored, and they may have a reflective coating inside.

❘ Fluorescent. These energy-efficient bulbs cast a diffuse, shadowless light that makes them great for general illumination. They are very energy efficient, but the old standard fluorescents are quite unflattering, making everything and everyone appear bluish and bland. Newer warm-white fluorescent bulbs render color in a way that more closely resembles sunlight. Fluorescents are available both in the familiar tube versions and in compact styles. In some parts of the country, local codes require fluorescent lights to conform to energy conservation mandates.

❘ Halogen. This is actually a type of incandescent lamp that operates at greater energy efficiency. It produces brighter, whiter light at a lower wattage. One disadvantage is a higher price tag. However, although halogens cost more up front, they last longer than conventional incandescents. Because a halogen bulb produces a higher heat output than other incandescents, it requires a special shielding. The low-voltage version of halogen bulbs produces a 50 percent brighter light than standard halogen bulbs. These are compact and use less electricity, which makes them more energy efficient, too.

❘ Xenon. Like halogens, xenon bulbs can be compact and produce a bright, white light that is very true to sunlight. But unlike halogens, which produce a lot of heat and emit harmful ultraviolet (UV) rays, xenon bulbs have low-heat output, making them more energy efficient.

❘❘ improved bulbs render better light ❘❘❘❘❘❘❘❘❘❘❘❘❘❘❘❘

ABOVE LEFT This fluorescent-lighted mirror supplies a diffused light that accurately renders color.

LEFT Xenon high-intensity discharge (HID) bulbs, developed for automobiles, are brighter than halogens and burn longer. This vanity strip is also dimmable.

||||| popular sconces come in many styles |||||||||||

OPPOSITE The polished-chrome mount for this halogen sconce has a sturdy 1950s look. The hand-blown shade resembles elegant Venetian glass.

LEFT A streamlined sconce provides a subtle wash of fluorescent light that is focused upward in a contemporary bathroom.

BELOW LEFT Set in distinctive satin-nickel bases, these halogen bulbs are covered by white-glass diffusers.

BELOW Torchère-style sconces with textured glass shades highlight the richness of an antique wood mirror.

lighting fixtures can set the stage

OPPOSITE In a large tub alcove, a chandelier produces both light and glamour. The fixture can be dimmed for mood lighting.

ABOVE LEFT Why restrict yourself to conventional light sources? This fanciful fixture adds panache as it sheds light on a vanity mirror.

ABOVE Sconces and table lamps that look like they belong in other rooms create accent and mood lighting.

LEFT Inspired by the richness of the Victorian-era, this bath boasts a period-style ceiling fixture for ambient light.

RIGHT Ventilation is particularly important in shower enclosures, which may require their own ventilation systems.

BELOW Windows surround a whirlpool tub, bathing it in light and opening to allow noxious fumes to flow out.

OPPOSITE BOTTOM Windows above the tub and in the shower aid air circulation in this bath.

ventilation

Adequate ventilation is a must in any humid environment, and you can't get much more humid than the modern bathroom retreat. Those fabulous home-spa features use more water than standard fixtures, raising the humidity level in the bathroom accordingly. The only solution is a good ventilation system. Ventilation combats the steam and condensation that causes mildew, rot, and deterioration of the bathroom's surfaces and the surrounding rooms or exterior walls of the house. If you haven't installed a proper moisture barrier between the bathroom and the exterior wall, you may face serious structural damage in addition to peeling and chipping paint. If you install glossy ceramic, stone, or glass tiles on bathroom surfaces, your ventilation needs are greater than if you installed an absorbent material, such as cork. (Unfortunately, many absorbent materials aren't appropriate for the bathroom because they can decay and spread bacteria.) Even glossy paints can resist absorption and create problems with mold and mildew. Beyond concerns for bathroom surfaces and structural elements, imagine the air quality in a stuffy and unventilated bathroom. Noxious fumes released into the air by cleaning solutions and grooming products, including hair spray and nail polish, pose a health risk. The most common side effects of this indoor air pollution include eye, nose, and throat irritation. Not exactly the kind of picture you had in mind when you dreamed of creating a relaxing, sybaritic haven in your new bathroom.

ventilating systems

There are three types of ventilation systems available for installation in a residential bathroom.

▌ **A recirculating fan.** As its name implies, a recirculating fan simply moves the air around in the room. It does not vent air to the outdoors, but it does help to dispel some of the moisture that has accumulated on surfaces during bathing.

▌ **A ducted system.** A ducted ventilation system discharges humidity in the bathroom by removing moist, stale air and odors and venting them through ductwork to the outdoors. Some of the latest options offered by manufacturers of bathroom fans include remote-location units, built-in lighting, units that include heaters, multiple speeds, quiet operation, and an automatic-on feature that is triggered by a device that senses high levels of humidity.

▌ **Room exhaust fans.** Separate exhaust fans mount anywhere on a ceiling or outer wall of a new bathroom. The main thing is to connect the fan to the outside via a vent cap on the roof or sidewall. To remove moist air and odors effectively from a bathroom, you need to match the fan capacity to the room's volume. Ventilating fans are sized by the number of cubic feet of air they move each minute (cfm). A fan should change all of the room's air at least eight times each hour. For 8-ft. ceilings, the following formula can help determine what you need:

$$\text{Fan capacity (cfm)} = \text{Room Width (ft.)} \times \text{Room Length (ft.)} \times 1.1$$

Fans are also rated in "sones" for the amount of noise they produce. A fan rated at 1 sone, the quietest, is about as loud as a refrigerator.

ABOVE In this bathroom an unobtrusive ceiling fixture combines overall illumination with a fan that whisks away humidity and odors.

OPPOSITE LEFT AND RIGHT Bathroom ventilation doesn't have to look industrial to be effective. Decorative ceiling fixtures such as these feature built-in fans and come in a variety of designs, sizes, and finishes.

Some time ago people said goodbye to the boring "necessary" room and happily greeted the bath of the twenty-first century, with its limitless opportunities for comfort, design, and personal expression. Restricted only by the size of their bathrooms—and the size of their budgets—homeowners are eagerly accepting these design opportunities. Whether your decorating style preferences run to traditional, nostalgic, high tech, or drop-dead glamorous, you'll find ideas for bringing them to life in your new bath with color and other special details in the pages that follow.

Get Stylish

‖ color ‖ trimwork and paneling ‖
‖ window treatments ‖
‖ style specifics ‖

All of the details, from the color palette to the trim, lighting fixtures, window treatment, art, and accessories, complement one another and enhance this bath's overall design scheme.

Color is probably your greatest decorating tool. Don't be afraid of it—it also happens to be one of the easiest things to change. So why do people typically stick with a neutral palette in the bathroom? A dated color on a permanent fixture can be expensive to change because usually you have to replace the fixture. However, special new paints make it possible to refurbish ceramic and porcelain with a new color for a fraction of the cost of replacement.

color

If you still want to stick with white or beige for the tub, sink, and toilet, introduce color to the walls or with accessories. Just pick up a can of paint and see how color can transform the space in no time at all. If you don't like what you've done, just grab another can of paint and start again. It's inexpensive and easy to apply.

One of the simplest things that you can do to test out a color is to apply it to a sheet of white poster board, hang it on the wall, and live with it a few days. Look at it during the day; then wait for evening and look at it again under varying levels of artificial light. Is the color still appealing to you? What effect does it have on the space at different times of the day? Even if you're thinking about tiling a wall or installing wallpaper, pick out the dominant color, find a matching paint, and apply this simple test.

LEFT Bold blue walls combine with white fixtures, panneling, and shelving to create an appealingly crisp look.

ABOVE Even a small amount of paint makes a big impact. Here, a swath of red paint rises above the off-white paneling. The matching curtains pull it all together.

LEFT Apple-green wainscoting and mauve walls look like they belong together in this bath.

❙ **ABOVE** The homeowners highlighted the charms of an older bath with vibrant green walls and a bold striped Roman shade.
❙
RIGHT Bright linens can intoduce color, too.

BELOW A wallcovering with a warm, neutral background brings a couple of bonuses to this bath—a sprightly border of birdcages and a charming trompe l'oeil window.

RIGHT You can use color to draw attention to handsome features in the room. Here, weathered copper fittings stand out against the reflection of acid-green glazed walls.

OPPOSITE RIGHT The unexpected use of bright color on the walls breathes vibrant life into a period-style bath, and looks particularly refreshing against the white of the fixtures and wainscoting.

paint and **w**allpaper

While you're thinking about color for the new bathroom, consider the types of paint, wallpaper, and fabric to use. Remember, bathrooms have lots of glossy surfaces, which reflect light. Unless you want an intense effect, use low-luster paints and matte finishes.

If you are concerned about moisture, especially in a room without ducted ventilation, shop for products that have been treated with mildewcide in the manufacturing process. Bathrooms are perfect breeding grounds for mold. When moisture seeps behind wallpaper, it creates a moldy, peeling mess. Luckily, this is a problem that can be avoided because there is a wide selection of products and glues that are designed specifically for bathroom applications.

ABOVE AND RIGHT   The rich wallcovering colors in this bath work with the architectural elements and furnishings to create an intriguing Old World ambiance. Trimmed with tile, the stone niche contains the shower.

OPPOSITE   A pale blue-gray background studded with luminous stars contributes to the serenity and calm of a master bathroom. The silver-toned mirror frame and wall sconce enhance the look.

choosing patterns

After you've settled on a color scheme, you can look for wallpaper and fabrics to carry through your theme. Two major factors in deciding which patterns to choose are the location and size of the room. Look at the adjoining areas, especially the ones that you must pass through to get to the bathroom. Think of them sequentially. If you want stripes in the bath but the adjoining hallway has a floral wallpaper, match the colors. In a small bathroom, a bold print may be too busy. On the other hand, it may be just what is needed to make an extralarge space feel cozy. Vertical designs will add height to a room. Conversely, horizontal motifs will draw the eye around it. In general, patterned wallpaper looks best in a traditional-style decor. In a contemporary scheme, subtle patterns that don't detract from the architecture and the materials are best. And avoid trendy looks, unless you want to make changes every couple of years.

bright idea

paint or paper?

ABOVE For a nautical effect, this bath combines a painted sea-and-sky mural on the walls, porthole-style mirrors, and ship's lamps.

Too busy to paint special effects? Not to worry—shop for a wallpaper that mimics the look.

RIGHT TOP TO BOTTOM Trompe l'oeil birds over a painted-sky background make this bath feel like perennial spring.

❙ try your hand at a painted effect

1 Brush on paint

To create sky, apply blue paint over a dry base coat. Let it dry. Then working at a 45-degree angle, slap on white paint using short, random strokes from a 4-in.-wide decorator brush. Pull the paint out until it's thin in some areas, and overlay it in others for an uneven color overall. Leave the tops of walls and the centers of ceilings more blue.

2 Mottle the paint

If you look at clouds as they appear in the sky naturally, they aren't uniform and the blue tones are varied. To re-create that look, work the wet paint to make it appear mottled (as it looks in the photo, above). Then step back and look at it. You'll notice that the mottling begins to suggest where you should place the clouds.

3 Establish clouds

Use a 2-in.-wide decorator brush tipped with the white paint to establish cloud shapes in the light sections. Apply random, flowing strokes to smooth and blend the colors.

4 Apply a thin wash

For a soft final finish, mix 8 parts water with 1 part white paint to make a thin wash, and brush it over the entire surface to break up the blue. Let it dry.

painting stripes

Stripes are among the most attractive painted effects you can add to a surface. Alternating broad and thin stripes, such as the ones used in the bathrooom above, can go on fairly quickly and evenly. If your hand isn't particularly steady, you may want to roll on the paint rather than use a brush to apply it. You can find narrow rollers in paint and craft shops, or you can cut down a standard-size roller to the desired width of the stripe. It's best to use a thick paint because you have to make one uninterrupted pass with the roller. Avoid running the roller up and down.

Load the roller from a paint tray. Start at the top, and run the roller straight down (or across) the surface. For a neat look, mask the edges before applying the paint.

LEFT Painted on the walls, stripes add both design distinction and the illusion of height.

RIGHT A crackle finish gives this beadboard a charming weathered look.

BELOW LEFT AND RIGHT Ragging and glazing provide texture and enhance the warmth of the soft wall color. Sponge-painted leaves decorate the ceiling.

trimwork and paneling

Architectural trim—a category that includes door and window casings, moldings, baseboards, and columns—is the crowning glory of a well-planned room, like a ribbon that puts the final beautifying touches on a gift package. It's important that you choose ornamentation that matches the style and proportions of your bathroom and the architecture of your house. Choices vary from simple to elaborate, as the drawings below illustrate. Ornate detailing works well in traditional rooms; simpler trim is more suitable for casual or contemporary settings. If you're after a really fancy effect, you may have to enlist a trim carpenter, but check your lumberyard or home center for precut or ready-made possibilities that are easy to install.

A paneled wainscot is another option for decoration. Use it to cover the lower half of the wall from the top of the baseboard to chair rail height or higher. Embellish it with molding or cap it with a wide shelf or ledge. Paneling is a way to hide minor imperfections in the wall, too. And thanks to modern engineering, some of today's paneling products and paint primers solve the problems that traditional wood paneling often presents when it's exposed to moist conditions.

popular trimwork profiles

Greek and Roman details are a part of so many decorating styles that it's hard to find ornamental trim without some kind of classical design. The ogee shape, for instance, appears on everything from interior trimwork to exterior cornices to table edges. Here are some of the basic molding shapes and motifs that have withstood the test of time.

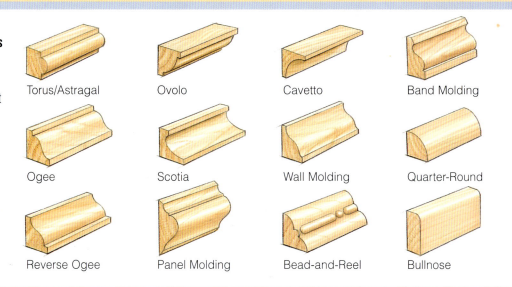

Torus/Astragal	Ovolo	Cavetto	Band Molding
Ogee	Scotia	Wall Molding	Quarter-Round
Reverse Ogee	Panel Molding	Bead-and-Reel	Bullnose

LEFT Bellyband casings with rosette corner blocks lend architectural distinction to these windows.

ABOVE For a classic country look, install white beadboard wainscoting and top it off with a strip of molding.

BELOW Something as simple as wood paneling painted a warm brown can produce a feeling of richness.

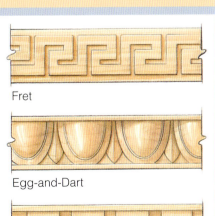

Fret

Egg-and-Dart

Dentil

LEFT Pierced and carved designs on the wood panel just below the crown molding in this bathroom add another layer of distinction to this architecurally pleasing design.

BELOW In a traditional bathroom, classic fluted pilasters contribute grace and style.

classic columns

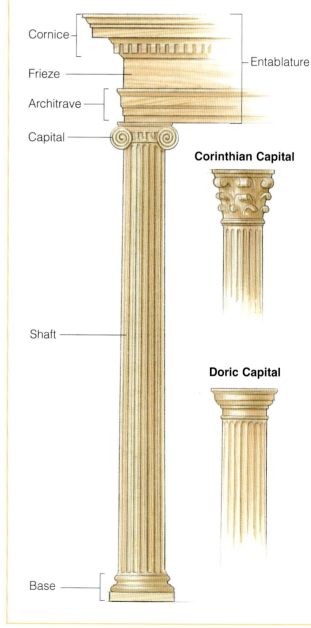

Ionic Column with Entablatures

Cornice

Frieze

Architrave

Capital

Entablature

Corinthian Capital

Shaft

Doric Capital

Base

RIGHT The opulence of this room is enhanced by ornate molding, walls of mirror, and a stenciled palm tree.

BELOW Here, a decorative column dignifies a gracious bathroom design.

Pilaster Construction

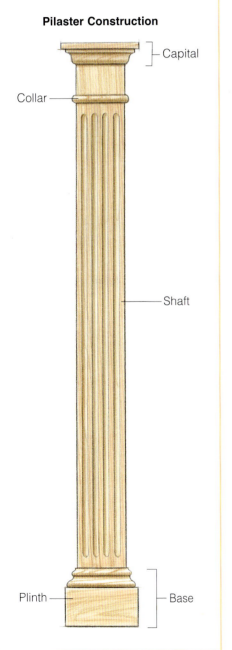

Capital

Collar

Shaft

Plinth — Base

door and **w**indow **c**asings

VICTORIAN-STYLE MITERED CASING

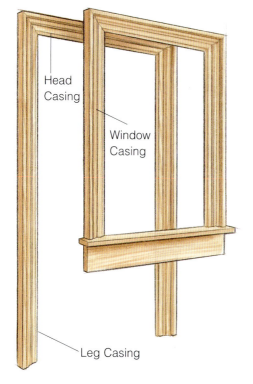

Head Casing

Window Casing

Leg Casing

BELLYBAND CASING WITH ROSETTE

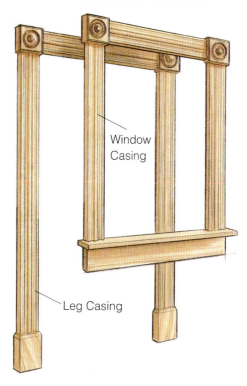

Window Casing

Leg Casing

ARTS AND CRAFTS–STYLE CASING

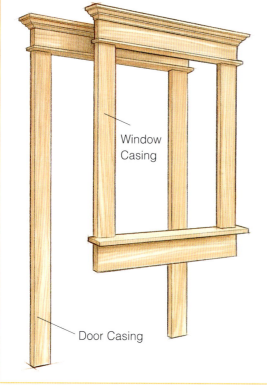

Window Casing

Door Casing

FLUTED CASINGS WITH DECORATIVE HEAD

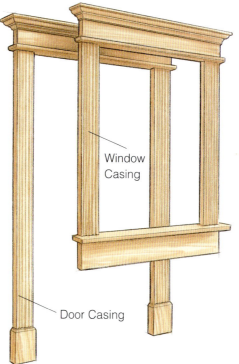

Window Casing

Door Casing

LEFT In this bath, the homeowners dressed up a plain-Jane casement window with a billowy curtain and simple mitered casings.

ABOVE Here, both trimwork and ceramic tile trim pieces add panache.

BELOW The richness of the paneled tub surround is echoed in this room by the window trim and crown moldings.

Choose a window treatment and control system that will both enhance your comfort while in the bathroom and help create the design expression that you are seeking. You can take your first cue from the climate where you live. In a hot climate, window treatments should block heavy direct sunlight, especially if the room faces south or west. In a cool climate, you'll need insulated window treatments to block drafts during the winter, especially if the bathroom faces north. Next consider privacy. If your bath window is visible from the yard or neighboring house, choose a device that can be easily closed to block all views to the interior. Your final selection will have to accommodate the type and size of your windows, the appearance you want, and your budget. Of course, for the bath, it's always best to choose easy-clean materials.

window treatments

LEFT If privacy isn't an issue, there is no better finishing touch for a country bath than filmy white café curtains hung from a decorative rod.

ABOVE Standard horizontal-slat blinds suit the traditional look of this older bath and can be easily adjusted to suit the time of day.

ABOVE RIGHT In addition to adding charm, wooden shutters with adjustable slats safeguard privacy while admitting light and air.

RIGHT A fabric roll-up shade is a pretty way to provide privacy. This one can be easily removed from the tension rod for cleaning.

window treatments add a finishing touch ||||||||||||||||||||||||

OPPOSITE In a bath with traditional style, a tie-back curtain at the window provides a soft touch of elegance and doesn't obstruct the use of the window crank.

FAR LEFT As illustrated by this curtain-and-wallcovering duo, two different patterns can harmonize side by side if they have colors in common.

LEFT Understated pleated shades suit the streamlined look of casement windows and can stand alone on style or pair harmoniously with a fabric treatment.

BELOW LEFT Neat and tailored Roman shades can be raised or lowered easily.

BELOW In an older house, a tall window admits abundant light; solid-panel wood shutters on the lower half close for privacy.

ALL PHOTOGRAPHS Which one of these decorating styles speaks most persuasively to you? Is it the refreshing simplicity of a cottage-style country design, **LEFT;** the rich, slightly formal graciousness of the traditional style, **BELOW;** the restrained nostalgia of the new Victorian approach, **OPPOSITE TOP;** the pared-down sleekness of the contemporary sensibility, **OPPOSITE BOTTOM LEFT;** or the ageless elegance of an Old World design, **OPPOSITE BELOW RIGHT?**

The bath is a place where you can express your personal style. There are no rules, but styles do fall into several categories, one of which is sure to please you. In a contemporary bath, the mood is serene; fixtures, fittings, and cabinets are clean-lined and unembellished; and there is an emphasis on natural materials, such as stone, glass, and even metal. A traditional bath design relies on finely detailed cabinets in cherry or mahogany, rich, deep colors, and polished metal fittings to set a gracious and elegant tone. A country-style bath, often equipped with vintage-look tubs or pedestal lavs, is cheerier and more casual. Cottage country is casual, too, but a bit more subdued, focusing on soft pastels, faded fabrics, and gauzy curtains rather than the brighter colors of country. In both styles, however, white-painted or light cabinetry, distressed furniture, wicker pieces, baskets, and framed prints figure prominently. The key to Old World style is "old." All of the elements—mellow wood and rich shades of ochre, rust red, and olive green—should look like they've seen a lot of use but are not yet shabby. The new take on Victorian may include period-style fixtures and fittings, but the cabinets, surfaces, window treatments, and accessories will be less fussy than in the past.

style specifics

| | | | | | | | | | | | | contemporary modern | | | | | | | | | | | | | | | | | | | | | | | | |

THIS PAGE Some of the fixtures and accessories you might choose to underscore this design theme—a sleek light fixture with a bright halogen bulb, ABOVE LEFT; a trendy above-counter sink with unique hand-forged fittings, ABOVE RIGHT; or an ultra-streamlined faucet in stainless steel, BELOW.

OPPOSITE This bathroom displays several of the hallmarks of contemporary modern design—a lack of embellishment, an overall streamlined look, large expanses of mirror, and the use of natural materials, such as stone, metal, and glass.

bright idea

a good fit

To be sure the faucet you like will flow into the lav you love at the right angle, buy them at the same time.

bright idea

no-fuss finish

If water spots and smudges on your faucets drive you crazy, choose a satin finish instead of a polished one.

OPPOSITE Mellow wood cabinets with the look of fine furniture set the stage for the traditional look.

LEFT To add updated elegance, you might choose faucets in a satin brass finish.

BELOW LEFT Typically used in a bedroom or hallway, wall lamps with fabric shades make gracious finishing touches in a bath.

BELOW Classic paneling and formal marble surfaces pull this look together.

traditional and timeless

country cottage casual

OPPOSITE A cousin of the enduring country style, cottage country emphasizes soft colors and a fresh, clean look.

ABOVE Vintage furniture is a cottage favorite.

RIGHT Charming old cabinets refreshed with white paint are also typical of the style.

BELOW Baskets are a staple of the style. These are beribboned and covered in linen.

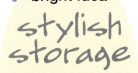

bright idea

stylish storage

Use decorated or fabric-covered baskets such as these to contain the clutter of seldom-used items.

old world

bright idea

the right stuff

Reinforce the
Old World atmosphere
with little extras
such as this
weathered urn.

OPPOSITE TOP A backdrop of stone-like ceramic tile helps to establish the Old World ambiance.

ABOVE LEFT A torchère-style wall sconce with a textured-glass shade and iron base has a vaguely medieval look, which is just right in an Old World-inspired room.

LEFT Accent tiles and border pieces have an aged look that is an essential element of the style.

ABOVE Mellow wood and ornate trim rev up the richness.

OPPOSITE A sleeker version of a period bathtub with fancy brass fittings injects Victoriana into this room, but apart from the stylized wallpaper and ornate mirror frame, the rest of the design is pure New Victorian—restrained and simple.

ABOVE RIGHT Prettily framed landscapes add interest but aren't over the top.

BELOW Handsome tilework is restricted to shades of gray stone.

new victorian

Resource Guide

MANUFACTURERS

Adagio, Inc.
www.adagio.bz
Makes hand-crafted sinks in a variety of materials.

American Standard
P.O. Box 6820
1 Centennial Plaza
Piscataway, NJ 08855
www.americanstandard-us.com
Manufactures plumbing and tile products.

Ann Sacks Tile & Stone, a div. of Kohler
8120 NE 33rd Dr.
Portland, OR 97211
800-278-8453
www.annsacks.com
Manufactures tile.

Armstrong World Industries
2500 Columbia Ave.
P.O. Box 3001
Lancaster, PA 17604
717-397-0611
www.armstrong.com
Manufactures floors, cabinets, ceilings, and ceramic tile.

Artemide
www.artemide.com
Manufactures lighting fixtures.

Bach Faucets
19701 DaVinci
Lake Forest, CA 92610
866-863-6584
www.bachfaucet.com
Manufactures faucets.

Bemis Manufacturing Co.
300 Mill St.
P.O. Box 901
Sheboygan Falls, WI 53085
800-558-7651
www.bemismfg.com
Manufactures toilet seats.

Benjamin Moore
51 Chestnut Ridge Rd.
Montvale, NJ 07645
www.benjaminmoore.com
Manufactures paint.

The following list of manufacturers and associations is meant to be a general guide to additional industry and product-related sources. It is not intended as a listing of products and manufacturers represented by the photographs in this book.

Corian, a div. of DuPont
800-426-7426
www.corian.com
Manufactures solid surfacing.

Dex Studios
404-753-0600
www.dexstudios.com
Creates custom concrete sinks, tubs, and countertops.

Formica Corp.
10155 Reading Rd.
Cincinnati, OH 45241
513-786-3525
www.formica.com
Manufactures plastic laminate and solid surfacing.

Ginger
460-N Greenway Industrial Dr.
Fort Mill, SC 29708
www.gingerco.com
Manufactures lighting and bathroom accessories.

Glidden
800-454-3336
www.glidden.com
Manufactures paint.

Herbeau Creations of America
3600 Westview Dr.
Naples, FL 34104
239-417-5368

www.herbeau.com
Makes vitreous china fixtures.

Hoesch Design
www.hoesch.de
Manufactures tubs and shower partitions.

Jacuzzi Whirlpool Bath
2121N. California Blvd.
Walnut Creek, CA 94596
800-288-4002
www.jacuzzi.com
Manufactures jetted tubs and showers.

Kohler
444 Highland Dr.
Kohler, WI 53044
800-456-4537
www.kohlerco.com
Manufactures plumbing products.

Resource Guide

KraftMaid Cabinetry
P.O. Box 1055
15535 South State Ave.
Middlefield, OH 44062
440-632-5333
www.kraftmaid.com
Manufactures cabinetry.

Lightology
1718 West Fullerton Ave.
Chicago, IL 60614
866-954-4489
www.lightology.com
Manufactures lighting fixtures.

MGS Progetti
www.mgsprogetti.com
Manufactures stainless steel faucets.

Merillat
www.merillat.com
Manufactures cabinets.

Moen
25300 Al Moen Dr.
North Olmsted, OH 44070
800-289-6636
www.moen.com
Manufactures sinks and faucets.

**Neo-Metro, a div. of
Acorn Engineering Co.**
P.O. Box 3527
City of Industry, CA 91744
800-591-9050
www.neo-metro.com
*Manufactures countertops, tubs, lavs,
and tile.*

NuTone, Inc.
4820 Red Bank Rd.
Cincinnati, OH 45227
888-336-3948
www.nutone.com
*Manufactures ventilation fans, medicine cabinets,
and lighting fixtures.*

Price Pfister, Inc.
19701 Da Vinci
Foothill Ranch, CA 92610
800-732-8238
www.pricepfister.com
Manufactures faucets.

Remcraft Lighting Products
P.O. Box 54-1487
Miami, FL 33054
www.remcraft.com
Manufactures lighting fixtures.

Robern, a div. of Kohler
701 North Wilson Ave.
Bristol, PA 19007
215-826-9800
www.robern.com
Manufactures medicine cabinets and accessories.

Seagull Lighting Products, Inc.
301 West Washington St.
Riverside, NJ 08075
856-764-0500
www.seagulllighting.com
Manufactures lighting fixtures.

Schonbek Worldwide Lighting, Inc.
61 Industrial Ave.
Plattsburgh, NY 12901
800-836-1892
www.schonbek.com
Manufactures crystal lighting fixtures.

Sharp
www.sharpusa.com
Manufactures consumer electronics.

Resource Guide

Sherwin-Williams
www.sherwinwilliams.com
Manufactures paint.

Sonoma Cast Stone
P.O. Box 1721
Sonoma, CA 95476
888-807-4234
www.sonomastone.com
Makes custom concrete sinks, pavers, tiles, and countertops.

Toto USA
1155 Southern Rd.
Morrow, GA 30260
770-282-8686
www.totousa.com
Manufactures toilets, bidets, sinks, and bathtubs.

Velux-America
800-888-3589
www.velux.com
Manufactures skylights and solar tunnels.

Villeroy and Boch
3 South Middlesex Ave
Monroe Township, NJ 08831
877-505-5350
www.villeroy-boch.com
Manufactures fixtures, fittings, and furniture.

Warmatowel, a div. of Sussman Lifestyle Group
43-20 34th St.
Long Island City, NY 11101
800-767-8236
www.sussmanlifestylegroup.com
Manufactures electric and hydronic towel warmers.

Watermark Designs, Ltd.
491 Wortman Ave.
Spring Creek, NY 11208
800-842-7277
www.watermark-designs.com
Manufactures faucets and lighting fixtures.

Waterworks
60 Backus Ave.
Danbury, CT 06810
800-998-2284
www.waterworks.com
Manufactures plumbing products.

Wilsonart International
P.O. Box 6110
Temple, TX 76503-6110
800-433-3222
www.wilsonart.com
Manufactures plastic laminate and solid surfacing.

Wood-Mode Fine Custom Cabinetry
1 Second St.
Kreamer, PA 17833
877-635-7500
www.wood-mode.com
Manufactures custom cabinetry.

Zodiaq, a div. of DuPont
www.zodiaq.com
800-426-7426
Manufactures quartz composite material.

ASSOCIATIONS

Ceramic Tile Institute of America (CTIOA)
12061 W. Jefferson Blvd.
Culver City, CA 90230-6219
310-574-7800
www.ctioa.org
A trade organization that promotes the ceramic tile industry. Its Web site provides consumer information about ceramic tile.

National Association of the Remodeling Industry (NARI)
780 Lee St. Ste. 200
Des Plaines, IL 60016
800-611-6274
www.nari.org
A professional organization for remodelers, contractors, and design-build professionals.

National Kitchen and Bath Association (NKBA)
687 Willow Grove St.
Hackettstown, NJ 07840
800-652-2776
www.nkba.org
A national trade organization for kitchen and bath professionals. It offers consumers product information and a referral service.

Tile Council of America, Inc
100 Clemson Research Blvd.
Anderson, SC 29625
864-646-8453
www.tileusa.com
A trade organization dedicated to promoting the tile industry. It also provides consumer information on selecting and installing tile.

Glossary

Absorption (light): The energy (wavelengths) not reflected by an object or substance. The color of a substance depends on the wavelength reflected.

Accent lighting: A type of light that highlights an area or object to emphasize that aspect of a room's character.

Accessible design: Design that accommodates persons with physical disabilities.

Accessories: Towel racks, soap dishes, and other items specifically designed for use in the bath.

Adaptable design: Design that can be easily changed to accommodate a person with disabilities.

Ambient light: General illumination that fills a room. There is no visible source of the light.

Antiscalding valve (pressure-balancing valve): A single-control fitting that contains a piston that automatically responds to changes in line water pressure to maintain temperature; the valve blocks abrupt drop or rise in temperature.

Apron: The front extension of a bathtub that runs from the rim to the floor.

Awning window: A window with a single framed-glass panel. It is hinged at the top to swing out when it is open.

Backlighting: Illumination coming from a source behind or at the side of an object.

Backsplash: The finish material that covers the wall behind a countertop. The backsplash can be attached to the countertop or separate from it.

Barrier-free fixtures: Fixtures specifically designed for disabled individuals who use wheelchairs or who have limited mobility.

Baseboard: A trim board attached as part of a base treatment to the bottom of a wall where it meets the floor.

Base cabinet: A cabinet that rests on the floor under a countertop or vanity.

Base plan: A map of an existing bathroom that shows detailed measurements and the location of fixtures and their permanent elements.

Basin: A shallow sink.

Bidet: A bowl-shaped fixture that supplies water for personal hygiene. It looks similar to a toilet.

Blanket insulation: Flexible insulation, such as fiberglass or mineral wool, that comes packaged in long rolls.

Blocking: A small piece of wood used to reinforce framing members.

Bridging: Lumber or metal installed in an X shape between floor joists to stabilize and position the joists.

Built-in: A cabinet, shelf, medicine chest, or other storage unit that is recessed into the wall.

Bump out: Living space created by cantilevering the floor and ceiling joists (or adding to a floor slab) and extending the exterior wall of a room.

Cable: One or more wires enclosed in protective plastic or metal sheathing.

Candlepower (Cp): The intensity of light measured at the light source.

Cantilever: A structural beam supported on one end. A cantilever can be used to support a bump out.

Casement window: A window that consists of one framed-glass panel that is hinged on the side. It swings outward from the opening at the turn of a crank.

Casing: The general term for any trim that surrounds a window.

Cement-based backer board: A rigid panel designed for use as a substrate for ceramic tiles in wet areas.

Centerline: The dissecting line through the center of an object, such as a sink.

CFM: An abbreviation that refers to the amount of cubic feet of air that is moved per minute by an exhaust fan.

Chair rail: A decorative wall molding installed midway between the floor and ceiling. Traditionally, chair rails protected walls from damage from chair backs.

Cleanout: A removable plug in a trap or drainpipe, which allows easy access for removing blockages.

Clearance: The amount of space between two fixtures, the centerlines of two fixtures, or a fixture and an obstacle, such as a wall. Clearances may be mandated by building codes.

Cleat: A piece of lumber fastened—to a joist or post, for example—as a support for other lumber.

Closet bend: A curved section of drain beneath the base of a toilet.

Closet flange: The rim of a closet bend used to attach the toilet drainpipe to the floor.

Code: A locally or nationally enforced mandate regarding structural design, materials, plumbing, or electrical systems that states what you can or cannot do when you build or remodel. Codes are intended to protect standards of health, safety, and land use.

Color rendition index (CRI): Measures the way a light source renders color. The higher the index number, the closer colors illuminated by the light source resemble how they appear in sunlight.

Combing: A painting technique that involves using a small device with teeth or grooves over a wet painted surface to create a grained effect.

Contemporary style: A style of decoration or architecture that is modern and pertains to what is current.

Cornice: Any molding or group of moldings used in the corner between a wall and a ceiling.

Correlated color temperature (CCT): A value assigned to a fluorescent lamp indicating the warmth or coolness of the light it produces.

Countertop: The work surface of a counter, usually 36 inches high. Common countertop materials include stone, plastic laminate, ceramic tile, concrete, and solid surfacing.

Cove lights: Lights that reflect upward, sometimes located on top of wall cabinets.

Crown molding: A decorative molding usually installed where the wall and ceiling meet.

Dimmer switch: A switch that can vary the intensity of the light source that it controls.

Door casing: The trim applied to a wall around the edge of a door frame.

Double-glazed window: A window consisting of two panes of glass separated by a space that contains air or argon gas. The space provides most of the insulation.

Double-hung window: A window that consists of two framed-glass panels that slide open vertically, guided by a metal or wood track.

Downlighting: A lighting technique that illuminates objects or areas from above.

Duct: A tube or passage for venting indoor air to the outside.

Enclosure: Any material used to form a shower or tub stall, such as glass, glass block, or a tile wall.

Escutcheon: A decorative plate that covers a hole in the wall in which the pipe stem or cartridge fits.

Faux painting: Various painting techniques that mimic wood, marble, and other stones.

Fittings: The plumbing devices that transport water to the fixtures. These can include showerheads, faucets, and spouts. Also pertains to hardware and some accessories, such as towel racks, soap dishes, and toilet-paper dispensers.

Fixed window: A window that cannot be opened. It is usually a decorative unit, such as a half-round or Palladian-style window.

Glossary

Fixture: Any fixed part of the structural design, such as tubs, bidets, toilets, and lavatories.

Fixture spacing: The amount of space included between ambient light fixtures to achieve an even field of illumination in a given area.

Fluorescent lamp: An energy-efficient light source made of a tube with an interior phosphorus coating that glows when energized by electricity.

Flux: The material applied to the surface of copper pipes and fittings when soldering to assist in the cleaning and bonding process.

Foot-candle (Fc): A unit that is used to measure the brightness produced by a lamp. A foot-candle is equal to one lumen per square foot of surface.

Form: The shape and structure of space or an object.

Full bath: A bath that includes a toilet, lavatory, and bathing fixtures, such as a tub or shower.

Furring: Wood strips used to level parts of a ceiling, wall, or floor before adding the finish surface. Also used to secure panels of rigid insulation. Sometimes called strapping.

Glass blocks: Decorative building blocks made of translucent glass used for non-load-bearing walls to allow passage of light.

Glazing (walls): A technique for applying a thinned, tinted wash of translucent color to a dry undercoat of paint.

Ground-fault circuit interrupter (GFCI): A safety circuit breaker that compares the amount of current entering a receptacle with the amount leaving. If there is a discrepancy of 0.005 volt, the GFCI breaks the circuit in a fraction of a second. GFCIs are required by the National Electrical Code in areas of the house that are subject to dampness.

Grout: A binder and filler applied in the joints between ceramic tile.

Half bath (powder room): A bathroom that contains only a toilet and a sink.

Halogen bulb: A bulb filled with halogen gas, a substance that causes the particles of tungsten to be redeposited onto the tungsten filament. This process extends the lamp's life and makes the light whiter and brighter.

Hardboard: Manufactured pressed-wood panels; hardboard is rejected by some manufacturers as an acceptable substrate for resilient and tile floors.

Highlight: The lightest tone in a room.

Incandescent lamp: A bulb that contains a conductive filament through which current flows. The current reacts with an inert gas inside the bulb, which makes the filament glow.

Intensity: Strength of a color.

Jamb: The frame around a window or door.

Jets: Nozzles installed behind the walls of tubs or showers that pump out pressurized streams of water.

Joist: Set in a parallel fashion, these framing members support the boards of a ceiling or a floor.

Junction box: Electrical box in which all standard wiring splices and connections are made.

Lavatory or lav: A fixed bowl or basin with running water and a drainpipe that is used for washing.

Load-bearing wall: A wall that supports a structure's vertical load. Openings in any load-bearing wall must be reinforced to carry the live and dead weight of the structure's load.

Low-voltage lights: Lights that operate on 12 to 50 volts rather than the standard 120 volts.

Lumen: A term that refers to the intensity of light measured at a light source that is used for general or ambient lighting.

Medallion: A decorative, usually round relief, carving applied to a wall.

Molding: Decorative strips of wood or plastic used in various kinds of trimwork.

Muntins: Framing members of a window that divide the panes of glass.

Nonbearing wall: A wall that does not support the weight of areas above it.

On center: A point of reference for measuring. For example, 16 inches on center means 16 inches from the center of one framing member to the center of the next.

Overflow: An outlet positioned in a tub or sink that allows water to escape if a faucet is left open.

Palette: A range of colors that complement each other.

Pedestal: A stand-alone lavatory with a basin and supporting column in one piece.

Pilaster: A vertical relief molding attached to a wall, usually made to resemble the surface of a pillar.

Pocket door: A door that opens by sliding inside the wall, as opposed to a conventional door that opens into a room.

Pressure-balancing valve: Also known as a surge protector or antiscalding device. It is a control that prevents surges of hot or cold water in faucets by equalizing the amounts of hot and cold water pumped out at any time.

Proportion: The relationship of one object to another.

Radiant floor heat: A type of heating that is brought into a room via electrical wire or pipes (to carry hot water) that have been installed under the floor. As the pipes or electrical wire heats up, the flooring material warms and heat rises into the room.

Ragging: A painting technique that uses a crumbled piece of cloth to apply or remove small amounts of wet paint to create a pattern or texture.

Rail: Horizontal trimwork installed on a wall between the cornice and base trim. It may stand alone, as a chair rail, or be part of a larger framework.

Reflectance levels: The amount of light that is reflected from a colored surface, such as a tile wall or painted surface.

Resilient flooring: Thin floor coverings composed of materials such as vinyl, rubber, cork, or linoleum. Comes in a wide range of colors and patterns in both tile and sheet forms.

Rigid foam: Insulating boards composed of polystyrene or polyisocyanurate that may be foil backed. Rigid insulation offers the highest R-value per inch of thickness.

Roof window: A horizontal window that is installed on the roof. Roof windows are ventilating.

Roughing-in: The installation of the water-supply and DWV pipes before the fixtures are in place.

Rubber float: A flat, rubber-faced tool used to apply grout.

Scale: The size of a room or object.

Schematic: A detailed diagram of systems within a home.

Sconce: A decorative wall bracket, sometimes made of iron or glass, that shields a bulb.

Sight line: The natural line of sight the eye travels when looking into or around a room.

Sister joist: A reinforcing joist added to the side of a cut or damaged joist for additional support.

Skylight: A framed opening in the roof that admits sunlight into the house. It can be covered with either a flat glass panel or a plastic dome.

Sliding window: Similar to a double-hung window turned on its side. The glass panels slide horizontally.

Snap-in grilles: Ready-made rectangular and diamond-pattern grilles that snap into a window sash and create the look of a

Glossary

true divided-light window.

Soffit: A boxed-in area just below the ceiling and above the vanity.

Soil stack: The main vertical pipe in a house that carries waste to the sewer or septic lines.

Spa: An in-ground or aboveground tublike structure or vessel that is equipped with whirlpool jets.

Space reconfiguration: A design term that is used to describe the reallocation of interior space without adding on.

Sponging: A paint technique that uses a small sponge to apply or remove small amounts of wet paint to create a pattern or texture on a surface.

Spout: The tube or pipe from which water gushes out of a faucet.

Spud washer: The large rubber ring placed over the drain hole of a two-piece toilet. The tank is placed over the spud washer.

Stencil: A design cut out of plastic or cardboard. When paint is applied to the cut-out area, the design will be reproduced on a surface.

Stippling: A decorative paint technique that involves applying paint to a wall with a stiff bristle brush.

Stock cabinets: Cabinets that are in stock or available quickly when ordered from a retail outlet.

Stops: On doors, the trim on the jamb that keeps the door from swinging through; on windows, the trim that covers the inside face of the jamb.

Stud: The vertical member of a frame wall placed at both ends and usually every 16 inches on center. A stud provides structural framing and facilitates covering with drywall or plywood.

Subfloor: The flooring applied directly to the floor joists on top of which the finished floor rests.

Surround: The enclosure and area around a tub or shower. A surround may include steps and a platform, as well as the tub itself.

Switch loop: Installation in which a switch is at the end of a circuit with one incoming power cable, and the outgoing neutral wire becomes a hot wire to control a fixture.

Task lighting: Lighting designed to illuminate a particular task, such as shaving.

Thickset: A layer of mortar that is more than ½-inch thick and is used as a base for setting ceramic tile.

Thinset: Any cement-based or organic adhesive applied in a layer less than

½-inch thick that is used for setting tile.

Three-quarter bath: A bathroom that contains a toilet, sink, and shower.

Tone: The degree of lightness or darkness of a color.

Tongue-and-groove: Boards milled with a protruding tongue on one edge and a slot on the other for a tight fit on flooring and paneling.

Traditional style: A style of decoration or architecture (typically of the eighteenth and nineteenth centuries) that employs forms that have been repeated for generations without major changes.

Trap: A section of curved pipe that forms a seal against sewer gas when it is filled with water.

Tripwaste: A lever-controlled bathtub drain stopper.

Trompe l'oeil: French for "fool the eye." A paint technique that creates a photographically real illusion of space or objects.

True divided-light window: A window composed of multiple glass panes that are divided by and held together by muntins.

Universal design: Products and designs that are easy to use by people of all ages, heights, and varying physical abilities.

Vanity: The countertop and cabinet unit that supports a sink. The vanity is usually included in the bathroom for storage purposes. It may also be used as a dressing table.

Vapor retarder: A material used to prevent water vapor from moving from one area into another or into a building material.

Vent stack: The main vertical vent pipe in the DWV system.

Ventilation: The process of removing or supplying air to a certain space.

Watt: The unit of measurement of electrical power required or consumed by a fixture or appliance.

Wax ring: A wax seal between the base of a toilet and the closet flange that prevents leaking.

Whirlpool: A special tub that includes motorized jets behind the walls of the tub for water massages.

Window stool: The horizontal surface installed below the sash of a window, often called a windowsill.

Wire connector: A small cap used for twisting two or more wires together.

Xenon bulb: A bulb similar to a halogen bulb, except that it is filled with xenon gas and does not emit ultraviolet (UV) rays. In addition, it is cooler and more energy efficient.

Index

Index

Index

Photo Credits

T: Top R: Right B: Bottom L: Left C: Center

All photography by Mark Samu, unless otherwise noted.

page 1: courtesy of Hearst Magazines page 3: design: Len Kurkowski, A.I.A. page 4: design: Sherrill Canet page 6: courtesy of Hearst Magazines page 8: builder: T. Michaels Contracting page 10: (*TL*) builder: T. Michaels Contracting page 12: builder: Witt Construction, design: Kitchen Dimensions page 13: design: Lee Najman pages 14–15: courtesy of Hearst Magazines pages 16–17: (*top row*) design: Chester Winthrop; (*all others*) design: Lucianna Samu pages 18–19: (*C*) courtesy of Hearst Magazines; (*R*) design: Sam Scofield, A.I.A.; (*BL*) builder: Bonacio Construction; (*C*) courtesy of KraftMaid; (*TL*) Len Kurkowski, A.I.A. page 20: courtesy of Hearst Magazines page 21: (*T*) design: Chester Winthrop; (*B*) design: Ken Kelly page 22: courtesy of Hearst Magazines page 25: courtesy of Hearst Magazines page 26: courtesy of Hearst Magazines, design: Carolyn Miller page 28: (*T*) design: Lee Najman; (*B*) builder: Witt Construction page 29: Kitty McCoy, A.I.A. page 30: courtesy of Hearst Magazines page 33: courtesy of Hearst Magazines page 34: design: Len Kurkowski, A.I.A page 36: (*T, BR*) design: Anne Tarasoff; (*BL*) design: Lee Najman page 37: (*T*) design: The Tile Studio; (*B*) courtesy of Hearst Magazines, design: Doug Moyer, A.I.A. page 38: (*B*) courtesy of Kohler page 39: (*T*) courtesy of American Standard; (*BR*) design: Lucianna Samu; (*BL*) courtesy of Hearst Magazines page 40: (*TL*) courtesy of Hearst Magazines; (*TR*) design: Bruce Nagel, A.I.A.; (*BL*) design: Peter Cook, A.I.A. page 41: (*T*) design: Doug Moyer, A.I.A.; (*B*) courtesy of Jacuzzi pages 42–43: (*TC*) courtesy of Hearst Magazines; (*BR, BL*) courtesy of Hoesch; (*TL*) courtesy of Kohler pages 44–45: (*TL*) cour-

tesy of Kohler; (*TR*) design: Jeanne Leonard; (*BR, BL, TL*) courtesy of Kohler page 46: (*T*) courtesy of Hearst Magazines page 47: (*T*) design: Lee Najman; (*B*) design: Ken Kelly page 48: (*TL*) courtesy of Jacuzzi; (*TR*) courtesy of Kohler; (*BL*) courtesy of Hearst Magazines page 49: courtesy of Kohler pages 50–51: (*TR*) design: TLK Interiors; (*BR*) architect: SD Atelier, A.I.A.; (*BC*) courtesy of Price Pfister; (*L*) design: Ken Kelly page 52: (*T*) courtesy of Price Pfister; (*B*) courtesy of Sonoma page 53: (*T*) courtesy of Hearst Magazines; (*BR*) courtesy of American Standard; (*BL*) courtesy of Price Pfister pages 54–55: (*TL*) courtesy of REHAU; (*TR*) courtesy of Kohler; (*BR*) courtesy of Sharp; (*BC*) courtesy of Warmatowel; (*BL*) courtesy of Kohler page 56: design: Lucianna Samu pages 58–59: (*TL*) design: The Tile Studio; (*TR*) design: Lee Najman; (*BR, BRC*) courtesy of Hearst Magazines; (*BLC*) design: Jeanne Leonard; (*BL*) courtesy of Hearst Magazines page 60: courtesy of Hearst Magazines page 61: (*TL*) design: Lee Najman; (*TR*) courtesy of Hearst Magazines; (*BR*) design: Jeanne Leonard page 62: (*TL*) courtesy of Hearst Magazines; (*TR*) design: The Tile Studio; (*BC*) design: Jeanne Leonard; (*BL*) design: Lucianna Samu/Benjamin Moore page 63: (*T*) design: Ken Kelly page 64: (*TL*) design: The Tile Studio; (*TR*) design: Sherrill Canet; (*B*) design: The Tile Studio page 65: (*T*) design: Jeanne Leonard pages 66–67: (*TC*) design: Sherrill Canet; (*BC*) courtesy of Hearst Magazines pages 68–69: (*C, TR*) courtesy of Robern; (*BR*) design: SD Atelier, A.I.A.; (*tile silhouettes*) courtesy of Waterworks page 70: courtesy of Ceramic Tiles of Italy page 71: courtesy of Kohler page 72: (*T*) courtesy of Sonoma; (*C, BR, BL*) courtesy of DEX Studios page 73: courtesy of Hearst Magazines pages 74–75: (*TC, BR*) courtesy of DEX Studios; (*BC*) courtesy of Sonoma; (*BL*) courtesy of DEX Studios;

(*LC*) courtesy of Sonoma; (*TL*) courtesy of DEX Studios page 76: (*T*) courtesy of Corian; (*BR*) www.davidduncan-livingston.com; (*BL*) courtesy of Corian page 77: (*T*) courtesy of Wilsonart; (*B*) courtesy of Zodiaq page 78: courtesy of Hearst Magazines page 79: (*T*) courtesy of Zodiaq; (*BR, BL*) courtesy of KraftMaid page 80: (*TL*) courtesy of Formica; (*TR*) design: Lucianna Samu; (*B*) courtesy of Armstrong page 81: design: Benjamin Moore pages 82–83: (*TL*) builder: Bonacio Construction; (*BC*) courtesy of Hearst Magazines page 84: (*T, B*) courtesy of Frigo Design page 85: design: Lee Najman page 86: design: Bruce Nagle, A.I.A. pages 88–89: (*TL*) courtesy of Corian; (*TLC, TRC*) courtesy of Hearst Magazines; (*TR*) builder: Bonacio Construction; (*BR*) courtesy of Sonoma pages 90–91: (*TL*) courtesy of Sonoma; (*TLC*) design: Deidre Gatta; (*L*) design: The Tile Studio; (*BC*) courtesy of Hearst Magazines; (*BL*) courtesy of Sonoma pages 92–93: (*TC*) courtesy of Sonoma; (*BC*) builder: Dean Durst Construction; (*BL*) design: Jeanne Leonard; (*LC*) design: Lucianna Samu; (*TL*) design: Lucianna Samu/Benjamin Moore page 94: (*TL*) design: Sherrill Canet; (*BL*) courtesy of Kohler page 95: (*T*) design: Lucianna Samu; (*B*) courtesy of Adagio page 96: (*T*) design: Ken Kelly; (*B*) builder: Dean Durst Construction page 97: (*TR*) courtesy of Sonoma; (*B*) builder: Bonacio Construction pages 98–99: (*TL*) courtesy of Bach; (*TC*) courtesy of Kohler; (*TR*) courtesy of Sonoma; (*BR, BL*) courtesy of Kohler pages 100–101: (*TL*) courtesy of Sonoma; (*TLC*) courtesy of Bach; (*TRC*) courtesy of Watermark; (*TR, BR*) courtesy of Sonoma; (*BL*) courtesy of Watermark; (*C*) courtesy of Kohler pages 102–103: (*TC*) courtesy of Toto; (*BR*) courtesy of Neo-Metro; (*BC*) courtesy of Toto page 104: (*TL*) courtesy of Kohler; (*TR*) courtesy of Toto page 105:

courtesy of Toto **page 106:** (*TL*) courtesy of Kohler; (*TR*) courtesy of Neo-Metro; (*B*) courtesy of Herbeau **page 107:** (*TL*) courtesy of Neo-Metro; (*R*) courtesy of Herbeau; (*B*) courtesy of Neo-Metro **pages 108–109:** (*TL*) courtesy of Kohler; (*TC, TR*) courtesy of Bemis; (*bottom row*) courtesy of Moen **page 110:** courtesy of Villeroy & Boch **page 111:** (*L*) courtesy of Bemis; (*TR, BR*) courtesy of Toto **page 112:** design: Ken Kelly **page 114:** courtesy of Merillat **page 115:** (*T*) courtesy of Wood-Mode; (*BR*) design: Jeanne Leonard **pages 116–117:** (*TL*) design: Teri Seidman Interiors; (*TC*) courtesy of Hearst Magazines; (*TR*) courtesy of Merillat; (*BR*) design: Richard Schlesinger; (*BC*) design: The Tile Studio **page 118:** (*T*) design: Correia Design Ltd.; (*BR*) builder: T. Michaels Contracting; (*BL*) design: The Tile Studio **page 119:** (*L*) courtesy of Wood-Mode; (*R*) courtesy of Hearst Magazines **page 120:** (*R*) design: The Tile Studio; (*R*) design: Sherrill Canet **page 121:** (*TL, TR*) courtesy of Wood-Mode; (*BR, BL*) courtesy of KraftMaid **page 122:** (*BL*) courtesy of DEX Studios; (*BR*) courtesy of Hearst Magazines **page 123:** (*T*) courtesy of Merillat; (*B*) courtesy of KraftMaid **pages 124–125:** (*TR*) design: Teri Kronman; (*BC*) courtesy of Hearst Magazines; (*L*) design: Correia Designs Ltd. **page 126:** builder: T. Michaels Contracting **page 127:** (*TL, TR*) design: The Tile Studio; (*B*) design: Anne Tarasoff **pages 128–129:** (*TL*) design: Jeanne Leonard; (*BC*) design: Lucianna Sam; (*L*) design: Deidre Gatta **page 130:** (*T, B*) courtesy of Merillat **page 131:** (*T*) courtesy of Merillat; (*B*) courtesy of KraftMaid **page 132:** courtesy of Hearst Magazines **page 133:** (*T*) courtesy of Kraft-Maid; (*BL, BR*) courtesy of Hearst Magazines **page 134:** (*T*) courtesy of KraftMaid; (*B*) courtesy of Merillat **page 135:** (*TL*) courtesy of Merillat; (*R*) courtesy of Kraft-Maid; (*BL*) courtesy of Merillat **pages 136–137:** design: Ken Kelly **page 138:** (*T*)

courtesy of Hearst Magazines, design: Doug Moyer, A.I.A. **page 139:** courtesy of Wood-Mode **page 143:** (*TL*) courtesy of Robern; (*TR*) courtesy of Hearst Magazines; (*B*) Freeze Frame Studio/CH **page 144:** design: Sherrill Canet **page 146:** (*T*) design: Jeanne Leonard; (*B*) courtesy of Hearst Magazines **page 147:** design: Benjamin Moore **page 148:** (*T*) courtesy of Hearst Magazines; (*B*) courtesy of Robern **page 149:** (*T*) design: Chester Winthrop; (*B*) design: Lee Najman **page 150:** (*T*) design: Lee Najman; (*B*) design: Chester Winthrop **page 151:** (*L*) courtesy of Hearst Magazines; (*R*) courtesy of Velux America **page 152:** (*L*) design: Jeanne Leonard; (*R*) design: The Tile Studio **page 153:** design: Carol Meltzer **pages 154–155:** (*TL*) courtesy of Seagull Lighting; (*TC*) courtesy of Schonbek Worldwide Lighting, Inc., photo: Glenn Moody; (*R, BC*) design: Lee Najman **page 156:** (*T*) courtesy of DEX Studios; (*BL*) design: Doug Moyer, A.I.A. **page 157:** (*T*) courtesy of Robern **page 158:** (*TL*) courtesy of Hearst Magazines, design: Ellen Roche, A.I.A.; (*TR*) design: Len Kurkowski, A.I.A.; (*B*) design: Carolyn Miller **page 159:** builder: Dean Durst Construction **page 160:** (*TL*) courtesy of Lightology; (*TR*) courtesy of Artemide; (*BR*) courtesy of Lightology **pages 162–163:** (*TL*) courtesy of Remcraft; (*TC*) courtesy of Artemide; (*R*) courtesy of Seagull Lighting; (*BC*) courtesy of Lightology **page 164:** courtesy of Schonbek Worldwide Lighting, Inc., photo: Glenn Moody **page 165:** (*TL*) courtesy of Hearst Magazines; (*TR*) design: Carolyn Miller **page 167:** courtesy of Hearst Magazines **pages 168–169:** courtesy of NuTone **page 170:** design: Sherrill Canet **pages 172–173:** (*TC*) design: Sherrill Canet; (*TR*) courtesy of Glidden; (*BR*) design: Lucianna Samu; (*BC*) courtesy of Sherwin Williams; (*L*) courtesy of Hearst Magazines **pages 174–175:** (*TC*) builder: Dean Durst Construction; (*BR*) courtesy of Schonbek

Worldwide Lighting, Inc. **pages 176–177:** (*TL, inset*) builder: T. Michaels Contracting; (*R*) courtesy of York Wallcoverings **page 178:** (*L*) courtesy of Benjamin Moore; (*right row*) design: Deidre Gatta **page 179:** Don Wong/CH **page 180:** design: Custom Creations Interior Design **page 181:** (*T*) design: Deidre Gatta; (*BR, BL*) design: Benjamin Moore **pages 182–183:** (*TC*) design: Graber Window Fashions; (*TR*) courtesy of Hearst Magazines; (*BR*) design: Lucianna Samu **page 184:** (*T*) courtesy of Hearst Magazines **page 185:** (*B*) design: Bruce Nagle, A.I.A. **page 187:** (*L*) design: The Tile Studio; (*TR*) design: Courland Designs; (*B*) design: Jeanne Leonard **page 188:** George Ross/CH **page 189:** (*TL*) design: Mojo-Stumer, A.I.A.; (*TR, BR*) courtesy of Hearst Magazines **page 190:** (*L*) design: SD Atelier, A.I.A.; (*TR*) courtesy of Motif Designs; (*B*) courtesy of Hearst Magazines **page 191:** (*TL*) design: Ken Kelly; (*BR*) design: Doug Moyer, A.I.A. **page 192:** (*T*) design: KraftMaid; (*B*) courtesy of Hearst Magazines **page 193:** (*T*) design: Deidre Gatta; (*BR*) design: The Tile Studio; (*BL*) design: Lee Najman **page 194:** (*TL*) courtesy of Ginger; (*TR*) courtesy of Sonoma; (*BL*) courtesy of MGS **page 195:** design: Lee Najman **pages 196–197:** (*L*) courtesy of Hearst Magazines; (*T*) courtesy of Bach; (*BR*) builder: T. Michaels Contracting; (*BC*) courtesy of Seagull Lighting **page 198:** design: KraftMaid **page 199:** (*TL*) design: Mojo-Stumer, A.I.A.; (*BL*) courtesy of Hearst Magazines **pages 200–201:** design: The Tile Studio **pages 202–203:** design: Deidre Gatta **page 221:** design: Lucianna Samu **page 204:** courtesy of Sonoma **page 205:** design: Ken Kelly **page 207:** design: Lee Najman **page 209:** courtesy of Kohler

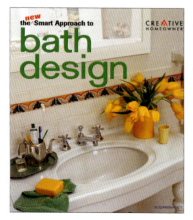
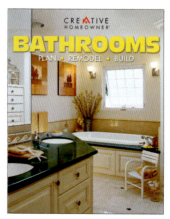